D1171518

LUCENT LIBRARY OF
BLACK HISTORY

AFRICAN AMERICAN
INVENTORS
Overcoming Challenges to Change America

By Sophie Washburne

Portions of this book originally appeared in
African American Inventors by Stephen Currie.

LUCENT
PRESS

Published in 2018 by
Lucent Press, an Imprint of Greenhaven Publishing, LLC
353 3rd Avenue
Suite 255
New York, NY 10010

Designer: Deanna Paternostro
Editor: Siyavush Saidian

Library of Congress Cataloging-in-Publication Data

Names: Washburne, Sophie, author.
Title: African American inventors : overcoming challenges to change America / Sophie Washburne.
Description: New York : Lucent Press, [2018] | Series: Library of Black history | Includes bibliographical references and index.
Identifiers: LCCN 2017004227 (print) | LCCN 2017008805 (ebook) | ISBN 9781534560710 (library bound book : alk. paper) | ISBN 9781534560727 (eBook)
Subjects: LCSH: African American inventors–Juvenile literature. | Inventions–United States–Juvenile literature.
Classification: LCC T39 .W37 2018 (print) | LCC T39 (ebook) | DDC 609.2/396073–dc23
LC record available at https://lccn.loc.gov/2017004227

Printed in the United States of America

CPSIA compliance information: Batch #BS17KL: For further information contact Greenhaven Publishing LLC, New York, New York at 1-844-317-7404.

Please visit our website, www.greenhavenpublishing.com. For a free color catalog of all our high-quality books, call toll free 1-844-317-7404 or fax 1-844-317-7405.

CONTENTS

FOREWORD

Black men and women in the United States have become successful in every field, but they have faced incredible challenges while striving for that success. They have overcome racial barriers, violent prejudice, and hostility on every side, all while continuing to advance technology, literature, the arts, and much more.

From medicine and law to sports and literature, African Americans have come to excel in every industry. However, the story of African Americans has often been one of prejudice and persecution. More than 300 years ago, Africans were taken in chains from their home and enslaved to work for the earliest American settlers. They suffered for more than two centuries under the brutal oppression of their owners, until the outbreak of the American Civil War in 1861. After the dust settled four years later and thousands of Americans—both black and white—had died in combat, slavery in the United States had been legally abolished. By the turn of the 20th century, with the help of the 13th, 14th, and 15th Amendments to the U.S. Constitution, African American men had finally won significant battles for the basic rights of citizenship. Then, with the passage of the groundbreaking Civil Rights Act of 1964, many people of all races began to believe that America was finally ready to start moving toward a more equal future.

These triumphs of human equality were achieved with help from brave social activists such as Frederick Douglass, Martin Luther King Jr., and Maya Angelou. They all experienced racial prejudice in their lifetimes and fought by writing, speaking, and peacefully acting against it. By exposing the suffering of the black community, they brought the United States together to try to remedy centuries' worth of wrongdoing. Today, it is important to learn about the history of African Americans and their experiences in modern America in order to work toward healing the divide that still exists in the United States. This series aims to give readers a deeper appreciation for and understanding of a part of the American story that is often left untold.

Even before the legal emancipation of slaves, black culture was thriving despite many attempts to suppress it. From the 1600s to the 1800s, slaves developed their own cultural perspective. From music, to language, to art, slaves began cultivating an identity that was completely unique. Soon after these slaves were granted citizenship and were integrated into American society, African American culture burst into the mainstream. New generations of authors, scholars, painters, and singers were born, and they spread an appreciation for black culture across America and the entire world. Studying the contributions of these talented individuals fosters a sense of optimism. Despite the cruel treatment and racist attitudes they faced, these men and women never gave up, changing the world with their determination and unique voice. Discovering the triumphs and tragedies of the oppressed allows readers to gain a clearer picture of American history and American cultural identity.

Here to help young readers with this discovery, this series offers a glimpse into the lives and accomplishments of some of the most important and influential African Americans across historical time periods. Titles examine primary source documents and quotes from contemporary thinkers and observers to provide a full and nuanced learning experience for readers. With thoroughly researched text, unique sidebars, and a carefully selected bibliography for further research, this series is an invaluable resource for young scholars. Moreover, it does not shy away from reconciling the brutality of the past with a sense of hopefulness for the future. This series provides critical tools for understanding more about how black history is a vital part of American history.

SETTING THE SCENE:

1857
United States Commissioner of Patents Joseph Holt rules that anything invented by a slave cannot be legally protected by a patent.

1777
Vermont becomes the first part of the United States to abolish the practice of slavery.

| 1777 | 1821 | 1857 | 1861–1865 | 1872 |

1821
Thomas Jennings becomes the first black man to be issued a patent by the U.S. government.

1872
Elijah McCoy is issued a patent for his innovative method for lubricating train engines.

1861–1865
The American Civil War is fought; President Abraham Lincoln emancipates all slaves; the 13th Amendment to the U.S. Constitution permanently abolishes slavery.

A TIMELINE

1880
Thomas Edison patents the common light bulb, sparking inventive interest in great minds of all races.

1915–1923
George Washington Carver investigates and discovers hundreds of uses for common agricultural products, including peanuts and sweet potatoes.

2005
Mark Dean leads a team that invents a computer capable of performing 280 trillion operations per second.

1880   1915–1923   1986   2005   2015

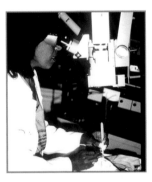

2015
Roland G. Fryer Jr. is awarded the John Bates Clark Medal, which is an award for outstanding contributions to the field of economics.

1986
Patricia Bath designs and invents a new device for laser eye surgery.

INTRODUCTION
A HISTORY OF INNOVATION

Despite using an uncountable number of important inventions every single day, few Americans are able to name many inventors. In fact, most people do not consider many everyday items to even be inventions. Most people could say that Wilbur and Orville Wright were the inventors of the airplane, because their invention has altered the very foundations of modern daily life. However, barely anyone can give as much information about other common items. Regardless of the vast improvements made to everyone's quality of life with each new invention, people generally do not care about the men and women who worked diligently to create them. This has been true for centuries.

Though few inventors get the credit they deserve, the stories of their technological innovations—and how they created them—are some of the most interesting in history. There is a proverb that has been used for hundreds of years: "Necessity is the mother of invention." It means that when something really needs to be improved, some great thinker or creator will come up with a new method of doing it. People needed to travel faster, leading to the invention of the airplane; people needed more efficient and effective light, leading to Thomas Edison's invention of the light bulb. There have been thousands of crucial inventions throughout the course of history, and every single one of them has an interesting story behind it. By investigating the need that prompts someone to become an inventor, it is possible to learn more about them, their time period, and the importance of their invention itself.

American history is full of inventors and their stories. Agriculture has been a critical part of life in North America since before Europeans even arrived.

Due to increasing demands for cash crops and profitability through the 18th century, numerous inventors came up with improved ways of farming. As new technology appeared, people competed over whose idea would be the best. Eli Whitney is the most famous of this era's innovators, and he is known to this day for his work during this time period. However, there were many other people who contributed to the strong technological improvements of early American life. Among these inventors were African Americans, many of whom were able to achieve a great deal even while enslaved. After the abolition of slavery, when many black citizens were able to acquire a real education, their work became even more impressive. Today, the legacy of invention in America, by people of all races, is celebrated across the world.

American Inventions and the World

The connections between inventors and the wider world are particularly strong in the case of African Americans. The lives and achievements of African American inventors over time not only show increasing improvement of technology, but they also function as snapshots, showing how African Americans were typically viewed in American society during specific historical eras.

Nearly all early black inventors were ignored or scorned by white Americans, who could not admit that African Americans were capable of matching whites in science and technology. Eventually, in the face of overwhelming evidence, white Americans began to accept that their black neighbors were just as capable of showing unusual talent and mechanical abilities as white people. However, for a long time, they still argued that these inventors were just outliers, and that the black race was still inferior. In more modern times, much of this prejudice has finally disappeared. African American inventors are now commonly accepted as valuable members of the scientific and cultural community.

Similarly, the stories of black inventors also help us understand the way that blacks have viewed themselves, as well as how they have functioned as a community through time. Because they have been social outcasts in America for centuries, many black inventors could not have accomplished what they did without the emotional, and sometimes financial, support of other African Americans. As the years have gone by, black inventors have increasingly drawn on this support and acknowledged the debt they owe to the larger black community as a whole. In addition, African American inventors have typically served as a point of pride for America's black citizens. Like African American writers, physicians, and athletes, they are examples of what black Americans can accomplish, even in the face of racial prejudice and hostility. In these ways, black inventors have encouraged and helped unify African Americans.

The history of black American inventors is largely about individual breakthroughs in science and technology. African American scientist George Washington Carver, for example, became famous for the hundreds of inventions he created out of peanuts and sweet potatoes. Any discussion of Carver acknowledges his brilliance, his total dedication to his work, and his valuable contributions to science. The same is true of other black inventors. From electrical expert Lewis Latimer to hair care entrepreneur Madam C.J. Walker, African Americans explored the same issues as their white counterparts, and sometimes had even more

George Washington Carver is one of the most respected scientists and creative thinkers in American history. His work with plants and plant products changed the way Americans lived.

PATENTLY UNFAIR

Just as authors and composers can copyright their books and music to prevent others from copying them, inventors can try to patent their inventions. In the United States, the federal government issues patents, which are official documents. They are frequently used to determine who was the first person to invent a particular device or procedure. More importantly, they give the first inventor the sole legal right to manufacture or to profit from their creation. In America, patent rights last for 20 years. During that time, no one other than the patent holder can produce or sell anything identical or very similar to the product described by the patent. Anyone who tries is considered to be infringing on the patent, and they can be sued in federal court.

Despite the protection offered by patenting an invention, not all inventors apply for one. Getting a patent can be a difficult and expensive process. The patent office charges fees for applications, applicants must hire artists to make detailed drawings of their creations, and attorneys are paid to advise applicants on legal matters. Even the simplest patent application requires inventors to fill out forms and keep track of the process. The patent system is sometimes criticized as being too complicated and expensive for anyone other than a rich inventor. People without much money or without the know-how to complete the forms generally never manage to patent their inventions. History shows that many African American inventors, in particular, have not been able to obtain patents for their work.

Patents are used throughout the world to protect inventions. The person who owns the patent can sue anyone who tries to illegally copy his or her designs.

success in finding solutions. Without exception, their tales of discovery are intriguing. Technologically speaking, these stories help explain how the world came to be the way it is. In human terms, they provide insight into how inventors work, think, and dream.

However, learning about African American inventors is about studying more than just their work. Although they were all certainly geniuses of science and discovery, they were also major African American figures in a white-dominated society. Their stories give us an understanding of what it was like to be black during their lifetimes. The story of Carver, for example, is not simply about one man's determination to find new uses for crops, nor is it simply the tale of a scholar pushing back the boundaries of science. Carver's story also reveals the difficulties faced by a black man in a world of prejudice, and it speaks to the desire of gifted African Americans to help the less fortunate among them. Similarly, though the story of Walker is partially about hair care, it is just as much about the pride African American women took in the success of someone like them, who had lived a hard life but had become a success. The life of Latimer reveals some subtle changes in the way white Americans viewed black Americans.

The stories of black inventors are not just stories about individual people, but stories about a people as a whole. At their most fundamental, they are stories about what it has meant—and what it still means—to be black in the United States.

CHAPTER ONE
PRE-CIVIL WAR BLACK INVENTORS

Well before the founding of the United States, people of African descent were living in European colonies in North America. Although slavery was an ancient practice, many places in Europe saw very little of it. With the exploration and colonization of the New World, however, the need for cheap labor saw a massive boom. As such, the settlers that came from England, France, and other European countries brought with them, or imported, African slaves. From the formation of what would eventually become the United States, there was a significant racial divide and significant prejudice. Nearly all the black residents of the colonies were there only as slaves. At this point in time, it was rare for them to even be considered people. They were treated like tools and property, rather than living humans, all across the colonies. Although some voices speaking for racial equality emerged after the official creation of the United States and the annexation of new lands, African Americans were still often mistreated.

For slave owners, the system of slavery continued to prosper for more than a century. Millions of Africans were abducted or sold from their homeland and enslaved in the United States. The trade was so widespread that the 1860 census—taken by the federal government just before the outbreak of the American Civil War—recorded nearly 4 million African slaves in America. That accounted for 13 percent of the entire population.

Around that same time, however, there were thousands of African Americans who had been freed from their enslavement. They mostly lived in the northern states, especially New York and Massachusetts.

However, even though they were free, they were not equal citizens according to the law. They were not allowed to vote, rarely had access to advanced education, and were still treated poorly by many whites. Only some people, who were called abolitionists because they supported the nationwide abolition of slavery, spoke out in defense of black people before the Civil War.

An Indiana minister and politician named James Mitchell said in the 1800s, "In casting the eye over the world, we find ... large masses of human beings of African origin; but we find little in those masses that is of [a superior] character."[1] This statement spoke for millions of Americans in the early 1800s, who believed that black people—slaves or free—were inferior to white people.

Inventing in Hard Times

Given these terrible circumstances, even attempting to invent anything was extremely difficult for African Americans of the pre–Civil War period. Slaves typically spent their days engaged in exhausting, repetitive farmwork that left little time or energy for the experimentation and tinkering that inventions generally require. Moreover, nearly all slaves were uneducated and knew little of the world outside of their plantation. Because they were still not considered citizens, slaves were not permitted to patent inventions or ideas. The strong racial prejudices of the time meant that even free blacks generally lacked the education, time, and resources to be inventors.

Although inventing was difficult for African Americans, it was not impossible. This was partly because of the relatively undeveloped technology at the time. While a scientific background is useful for any inventor, the world of the early 19th century was a simple place. Technologically speaking, the inventions of the period were simple as well. Developing a more efficient farm tool, for example, did not require a well-equipped laboratory or a Ph.D. in physics. It simply called for a sharp mind and a familiarity with farmwork. Nothing prevented African Americans, even slaves, from creating inventions such as these—and, in fact, many did exactly that.

For black people, slave or free, inventing could start them on a road to some success. In most fields, prejudiced whites ignored exceptional blacks. The average white American had no interest in the writings of black authors, for example. New inventions, however, were different.

A good invention could improve someone's life, reduce their workload, or increase their wealth. This was true regardless of race. By building a new machine or coming up with a clever new way of doing something, a free African American might have been able to actually make decent money. Additionally, a black inventor might have even achieved some respect from whites, however reluctantly.

It can be difficult to determine which inventions during this period were actually created by blacks. That is especially true for slaves, who could not apply for patents or make any legal claim to their inventions. Nothing prevented a slave owner from saying that a slave's discovery was actually their own, and it is likely that many masters did exactly that. While free blacks were certainly better off than slaves, they were not granted many legal protections either. Because of the biased judicial system, it was very challenging for an African American to fight against a white person in a legal battle. It is definitely possible that people stole the ideas of free African Americans, believing that they could get away with it unquestioned in court. As a result, at least some inventions patented by whites

before the Civil War may well have been the creations of black inventors instead.

Historical evidence supports this possibility. In particular, historians believe that one of the great inventions of the early 1800s might have been created at least in part by a slave. In 1834, a white farmer named Cyrus McCormick was issued a patent for a mechanical reaper. This machine was drawn by horses and used a series of cutting blades to harvest large quantities of crops quickly. It was an important innovation for the largely agricultural United States, and eventually the world, as it would reduce labor costs and increase crop yield. However, there is evidence that McCormick did not invent the groundbreaking machine on his own. He was reportedly assisted by one of his slaves, Jo Anderson. It is still not totally clear to historians how big Anderson's role was in the great success of McCormick's invention. Some sources suggest that Anderson's main function was simply to assist McCormick with basic tasks; as one writer pointed out, Anderson "is not recorded as claiming any significant role"[2] in the project. Other historians, however, believe that Anderson suggested ideas to McCormick, or even that Anderson was the person

Cyrus McCormick attained great wealth during his lifetime for inventing a mechnical reaper similar to this one. It is possible that a slave helped him come up with his ideas.

who did most of the work to make the mechanical reaper a reality.

A Slave's Solution

While no one knows precisely how much impact Jo Anderson had on the invention of the reaper, historians have documented several definitive cases of slaves inventing something new and important. One of the most famous of these slaves was a man named Benjamin Montgomery. Born in Virginia in 1819, Montgomery was owned for many years by Joseph Davis, whose brother Jefferson later became the president of the Confederate States of America during the Civil War. As a young adult, Montgomery was extremely capable and intelligent, and Joseph Davis gave Montgomery opportunities that were not available to the average slave. Montgomery demonstrated a particular talent for surveying and mechanics; Joseph Davis once wrote that Montgomery had "few Superiors as a Machinist [someone who works with heavy machinery]."[3]

In the late 1850s, Montgomery was living and working on one of Davis's plantations in Mississippi. With the large amount of river-based trade that occurred in that region, boats frequently traveled on the rivers near Davis's land. The water in these rivers, however, was often shallow, and the boats' rotating propellers sometimes snagged on the river bottom. This frequently caused boat wrecks or stoppages, slowing down the entire chain of distribution for merchants. Some products could spoil if the boat was trapped for too long. Although he was a slave, Montgomery was trusted enough to draw up a plan for a propeller that would be slanted slightly. Normally, propellers during this time were straight, vertical installations. The slant kept the propeller securely in the water, and the boat ride was smoother as well. "The blades cut into the water at an angle," one historian wrote, "causing less resistance and therefore less loss of power and jarring of the boat."[4] Montgomery soon built a working model of the propeller and attached it to a steamboat. It had exactly the effect he wanted.

Though Montgomery's invention is the most famous of the era, other slaves also came up with innovations of their own. In the early 1800s, a slave named Ebar developed a new way of manufacturing brooms in Massachusetts. Ned, a slave on a Mississippi plantation, developed a tool for scraping cotton in the 1850s. Ned's master was even willing to credit his slave for the invention. However, he also tried to patent the device in his own name by arguing that whatever a slave created was legally the property of the slave's owner. Government officials still denied the request. In North Carolina, a slave named Stephen Slade came up with an innovative way to dry tobacco leaves that changed their color to a bright yellow. This appealed to buyers and raised the prices his owner could charge. Numerous other slaves are mentioned in historical records as minor inventors, mainly creating new farm tools and household objects.

A Whale of an Invention

Slaves such as Montgomery and Slade, though talented and intelligent, were exceptions to the general trend. Free blacks made up the largest group of African Americans recognized as inventors in the pre-Civil War era. One of the most important of these inventors was a free black man named Lewis Temple. Born as a slave

JAMES FORTEN

Born in Philadelphia in 1766, James Forten was one of the best-known blacks of the early 1800s. An activist against slavery, a leader of Philadelphia's black community, and a highly successful businessman, Forten earned the respect of blacks and even some whites. He was apprenticed to a sailmaker at a young age and made his money by running a factory that produced sails. By some estimates, he earned well over $100,000 from this business. In the 19th century, this was an incredible fortune, especially for an African American.

In addition to his business sense and his work against slavery, Forten is sometimes remembered as an inventor. Many books on African American inventors claim that Forten developed and patented a device that made sails easier to operate. Although sources are vague about the details of the invention, including the year it was created, a few of these sources attribute the majority of Forten's earnings to this invention.

Although Forten may indeed have tried to improve sail technology, it seems doubtful that he invented anything that was truly new. "There is nothing to substantiate this [idea],"[1] Forten's biographer wrote, pointing out that no patent was ever issued to Forten or to any of his business partners. It is possible that he created a small fix to one aspect of sail design or use, but even if he did, he was never widely regarded as a revolutionary inventor. Forten, despite his great suc-

in Virginia in 1800, Temple moved to New Bedford, Massachusetts, as a young adult. He was eventually freed by the antislavery laws in the North. New Bedford was a major seaport, and it was known at the time as an important center for the whaling industry. Because whale oil was one of the primary sources of fuel in the 19th century, ships routinely set out from New Bedford to sail the sea in search of whales. If a ship caught and killed enough whales, its owners and crew could all make excellent money.

Finding, hunting, and killing a whale was difficult and dangerous. First, the crew had to maneuver close enough to the whale to strike it with a harpoon. A harpoon is a long, sharp spear with a long rope attached to the handle. As the ship got close to the whale, the crew had to throw their harpoons at it and hope that at least one of them stuck into its thick flesh.

cess as a businessman and a committed leader of his people, was probably not a great inventor.

1. Julie Winch, *A Gentleman of Color: The Life of James Forten.* New York, NY: Oxford University Press, 2002, p. 73.

James Forten, though not remembered for his innovations, was one of America's first successful black businessmen. He donated much of his money to the causes of abolition and improving black lives.

Unfortunately for the sailors, the harpoons of the 1820s and 1830s were not reliable. The spear tips were sharp enough to penetrate into the flesh of the whales, but they frequently fell out again once the injured and irritated whales started thrashing around in the water. If the harpoon fell out, the whale was able to swim to safety. The ineffective tips of the harpoons were costing sailors money and making their jobs more difficult.

One historian wrote that, by the early 1840s, "the urgent need of a new and better instrument [was becoming] daily apparent."[5]

Temple was an experienced blacksmith, but not a whaler himself. However, in the mid-1840s, he took on the challenge of designing a better harpoon. He spoke with whalers and sailors, who told him their complaints and experiences with unreliable harpoons. After experimenting with

SLAVES AND THE COTTON GIN

Cyrus McCormick's reaper was one of two revolutionary new farming machines developed and patented in the early years of the United States. The other was the cotton gin. One of the most well-known tools in U.S. history, it was a device that separated the fibers of the cotton plant from the seeds. This machine was patented in 1794 by a white man: Connecticut native Eli Whitney. Like McCormick's reaper, Whitney's machine accelerated a process that had previously been done slowly and by hand, saving time and energy. Moreover, it allowed farmers to produce a much larger crop. Whitney's ingenuity in the development of this device is certainly impressive. However, as with McCormick's reaper, African American slaves may deserve some of the credit as well.

It is well documented that Whitney visited several cotton plantations in Georgia before building his machine. Most historians agree that slaves on many plantations used crude, handmade tools of their own creation to separate cotton. Some historians believe that Whitney saw a number of these devices in action during his visits and adapted their basic principles into the machine that made him famous. "Slaves made certain appliances experimenting with the separation of the seed from cotton," wrote Henry E. Baker, a patent examiner in the early 1900s who had an interest in the inventions of African Americans, "which, when observed by Eli Whitney, were assembled by him as the cotton gin."[1] As with the mechanical reaper, the amount of influence of African Americans in the production of the cotton gin will probably never be known.

1. Quoted in Patricia Carter Sluby, *The Inventive Spirit of African Americans: Patented Ingenuity*. Santa Barbara, CA: Greenwood, 2004, p. 13.

various models, he created a unique whaling weapon. Its definitive feature was a movable spear tip. After the sailor threw it, the spear would pierce the whale's skin; then, with the pull of a secondary rope, the spearhead would pivot at a right angle and get stuck in the body of the whale. With this mechanism, called a toggle, it was almost impossible for the whale to

This is an example of a simple harpoon. Temple's toggling harpoon had additional metal points and a mechanism that was used to make it stick.

knock the harpoon loose. In addition, the toggling harpoon typically pierced deeper into the whale than the harpoons that preceded it. Where earlier harpoons caught onto the whale's skin and blubber, Temple's invention was designed to fasten itself to the muscle, which is one layer below that. This design also kept the harpoon firmly in place.

At first, potential clients were hesitant to accept Temple's new harpoon. Not only was he not a sailor, he was also a former slave. However, after a few whaling captains purchased—and had great success—with his invention, its popularity was widespread. He never patented his invention, and because of that, he was not able to reap all the rewards for his innovation. He did make enough money to open his own factory, though, and he received plenty of recognition for his work. Even without a patent, the invention quickly became known as the Temple toggle. Whalers who used the new harpoon saw that Temple's device dramatically increased their catch, and word spread throughout New Bedford and other whaling ports. Before long, whalers everywhere were using Temple's design. One early-20th century researcher concluded that "the Temple toggle was the most important single invention

BANNEKER OF BALTIMORE

Benjamin Banneker was a free African American who lived from 1731 to 1806. He was one of the most remarkable men, of any race, of his time. Though he is not credited with inventing anything original, he had many of the characteristics of an inventor: an inquiring mind, a passion for science, and an enthusiasm for machinery. He was interested in astronomy, and he created an almanac each year. In these almanacs, he calculated the times of sunsets, the phases of the moon, and other astronomical events. After analyzing the mechanism of a watch, he built what was probably the first clock ever constructed in the British North American colonies. He was a talented surveyor as well, and he was involved in the planning and construction of Washington, D.C.

Banneker, a free black man from Maryland, was aware that whites of his time held a very low opinion of African Americans, even those who were not enslaved. Moreover, he recognized that his abilities made him unusual among the blacks of his day, most of whom were uneducated and enslaved. Rather than attributing his success to natural talent, though, Banneker believed he was an example of what any African American could achieve if given the opportunity. He spent much of his life trying to change people's minds on the subject of African Americans, and he succeeded—to an extent. Though he did not live to see slavery abolished, Thomas Jefferson once wrote that Banneker was

in the whole history of whaling."[6]

From Farming to Carpentry

Prior to the Civil War, many other free blacks made names for themselves as inventors. In 1821, for example, Thomas Jennings of New York received what was probably the first patent ever granted by the United States to a black American. He was issued a patent for a new method of laundering clothes. His innovative techniques were expanded over the years and are now called dry cleaning. Roughly a decade later, Henry Blair of Maryland patented a tool for planting corn. In doing so, he became just the second black man to ever receive a patent by the American government. He followed up this success by developing a cotton planter that was also issued a patent. These new machines helped increase crop yield while cutting down on the growth strong evidence that the lack of achievement by African Americans "is merely the effect of their [poor treatment] and not ... from any difference in the [strength] of the parts [of the brain] on which intellect depends."[1]

1.Quoted in John Sibley Butler, *Entrepreneurship and Self-Help Among Black Americans: A Reconsideration of Race and Economics.* Albany, NY: State University of New York Press, 1991, p. 58.

Benjamin Banneker was one of the first great African American thinkers. He helped inspire future generations of black innovators, and he is an integral part of black history in America.

of weeds.

George Peake of Ohio was another early black inventor; though he was never issued any patents, he is credited with the development of a type of tool for grinding grain without heavy machinery. Called a hand mill, it reportedly allowed individuals to manually operate a small set of grinding wheels that produced higher quality ground meal. His hard work and ingenuity helped make him a "highly respected citizen"[7] among both whites and blacks in his home near Cleveland.

Another native of Ohio, Henry Boyd of Cincinnati, invented and produced a new design for bed frames around 1830. Boyd's design used a thin wooden rail to connect the bed's headboard and footboard, making it much sturdier than most contemporary models of bed frames. The bed was also unusual for using no iron bolts. Boyd was proud of his design and was quick to sell it on the open market. "This newly invented Bedstead," he wrote in a newspaper advertisement, "is [guaranteed] to be superior to any other ever offered in the West."[8]

Boyd's bed was an impressive achievement, doubly so when given the inventor's background. Born in Kentucky, Boyd had spent his first 18 years as a slave. He eventually purchased his freedom and moved to Ohio around 1820. Cincinnati was free territory, but the people of the city were not welcoming to black people. No one was willing to give him a job. An early account described what his life in Cincinnati was like: "Day after day did Henry Boyd offer his services from shop to shop, but [just] as often was he [sent away], generally with insult, and once with a *kick*."[9] Unwilling to give up, Boyd persevered, eventually finding work as a carpenter. After creating his bed design, he left his job to open his own factory.

In spite of, and possibly because of, his success, hostility toward Boyd remained. His factory was destroyed by fire at least twice; the fires were likely set by racist white residents of Cincinnati in an attempt to force him out of business. Boyd was also unable to ever patent his design. Some sources suggest that government officials told Boyd that patents were

not available to African Americans. Boyd's design was eventually patented by a cabinetmaker in Cincinnati, a white man named George Porter. Though there is no decisive evidence, historians speculate that Porter acted as Boyd's agent. This meant that Porter may have applied for the patent on Boyd's behalf to ensure that competitors could not copy the original design.

If this interpretation is accurate, however, Porter's attempt to keep Boyd's invention protected was unsuccessful. Other furniture makers, recognizing how clever Boyd's design was, ignored the patent and quickly manufactured beds based on the same principles. Even so, most of these beds were inferior. Boyd believed, however, that it was difficult for customers to distinguish his own products from those of other manufacturers. "Caution," Boyd warned shoppers in another advertisement for his product. "There are imitations of this Bedstead [on the] market very much resembling it."[10] In the end, Boyd stamped his name on his products so people could identify his as genuine. Even today, his beds are highly prized. In 2006, for instance, a Boyd original bed frame sold for more than $6,000.

Educated in France, Innovative in America

The free black inventors in the time before the Civil War had many things in common. Most were born in the North or in the slave states close to it. Often they were natives of Maryland, Ohio, Virginia, and Kentucky. Few had much formal education; some were even illiterate. Most knew little of the world beyond the eastern United States. There were, however, exceptions to whom these limitations did not apply. In particular, the most famous and successful black inventor of the time—a Louisiana scientist named Norbert Rillieux—was unique even among black inventors.

Born in March 1806, Rillieux grew up in the city of New Orleans. His father was a white man from France with a background in engineering. His mother was a former slave with three European grandparents and one grandparent of African descent. According to Louisiana law, however, that one grandparent was enough to categorize her as black. The same logic applied to newborn Norbert: "The prevailing legal definition of the period was that 'one drop' of African blood made a person 'negro' or 'colored.'"[11] As a result, though seven of his eight great-grandparents were white Europeans, his single African great-grandparent meant that, legally, the state viewed Norbert Rillieux as black, too.

By American standards at the time, New Orleans was a cosmopolitan city with a sizable free black community. Still, even in a relatively progressive city, racial prejudice was common. Hoping to shield their son from racism and give him a better education, Rillieux's parents elected to send him to school in France. There, he proved to be a thoughtful student and a hard worker. Upon finishing his education, he was hired to teach mechanics and engineering in Paris. He also pursued his own personal interests, doing research on the steam engine, which was a relatively new invention at the time.

Rillieux's work with the power of steam soon convinced him that the science and technology behind steam engines could be used in the processing of sugar, a major crop in his home state of Louisiana. Many farmers in the area planted sugarcane, an important source of sugar. Turning these plants into sugar that could be used by humans required several complicated steps. Just before the last step of the process, there was a liquid sugar solution. The final refinement required that the water in the solution be evaporated (turned into gas), which would leave only the sugar. In the early 1830s, this step utilized

*Norbert Rillieux was a great scientist and engineer.
His unique methods for multiple evaporation are still
used today.*

The Miracle of Multiple Evaporation

In 1833, Rillieux returned to New Orleans to work on the problem. His first ideas were not successful, but he persisted. Before long, he put together a model for a device that he called a multiple effect evaporator. According to his designs, the steam produced by the heated sugar solution was recycled and used to raise the heat of the solution even further. Thus, the water was boiled multiple times, giving the invention its name.

Though Rillieux's initial tests were mechanically promising, he did not have enough money to create a working model. After several years of unsuccessfully trying to convince wealthy Louisiana business leaders to support him, he managed to catch a break from a Louisiana planter named Judah Benjamin. Benjamin ran one of the most profitable sugar plantations in Louisiana, and he hired Rillieux to

a procedure known as the "Jamaica Train." To accomplish it, workers (generally slaves) poured the boiling hot solution back and forth between large kettles until the water was gone. Rillieux hypothesized that he could use steam as the basis for an improved system of evaporating water.

improve his farm's sugar production—which he did by installing his special evaporator. In 1843, after a decade of hard work, Rillieux patented the sugar industry's first multiple evaporator.

As with Lewis Temple's toggle harpoon, it was immediately clear that Rillieux's invention was a significant improvement over what had come before. The multiple evaporator saved time, cut costs, and even produced higher quality sugar. It was estimated that a large plantation could make nearly $15,000 in additional profits every year by using his machine. More importantly, because the machine captured and recycled the steam, which was incredibly hot, slaves and other workers were protected from major burns or other injuries in the process. Many sugar planters were eager to install one of the new multiple evaporators on their own farms. With production costs suddenly lower, sugar became more affordable and readily available to the average American. The benefits for Rillieux, personally, were also tremendous. As the patent holder, Rillieux received a share of the money from every evaporator sold in the United States. His wealth quickly rose to a level that few whites, and even fewer African Americans, could match.

Still, Rillieux wanted more than money as his reward. During the 1840s and 1850s, as the Civil War approached, the white majority in New Orleans became more and more hostile to African Americans. State and city leaders passed new laws that restricted black people in many ways. They had to follow a curfew and, in the mid-1850s, even free blacks were forced to carry passes to prove that they were not slaves. Rillieux was used to the freedoms of France and the relatively tolerant New Orleans of his youth. As such, he was deeply offended by these harsh and prejudicial measures. Moreover, although Rillieux continued to make money from his evaporator, he believed that many white American scientists and academics ignored him and his achievements simply because of his race. Over time, this discrimination made him angry and frustrated with his countrymen.

As a result, Rillieux turned his back on his native land in the late 1850s. He moved to France permanently, where he continued to invent and defend his patents. There is little question that Rillieux received better treatment in France than he had in America. However, he was still not satisfied with the recognition he received. Many French scientists were reluctant to admit that Rillieux's creations worked as well as they truly did. He died in 1894, and though he never felt he was given the respect he deserved, he had acquired enough money for his family to live comfortably after he had passed.

Though Rillieux's prestigious background distinguished him from other African American inventors of his time, in the end, he was equally incapable of escaping from American racism. Whether slave or free, educated or illiterate, trained scientist or gifted amateur, the fundamental truth for black inventors was the same. However clever their designs, however remarkable their work, they were African Americans first and inventors second. Norbert Rillieux's financial success could not buy him the respect he craved in a prejudicial society; Lewis Temple's redesigned harpoon enriched the white men who ran the whaling industry but did not increase his own wealth by the same amount; and despite Benjamin Montgomery's remarkable mechanical knowledge, he remained enslaved until the Civil War brought slavery to an end.

Still, the lives of these early black inventors demonstrated that African Americans could be just as creative and influential as anyone. Despite the hardships they faced, men such as Norbert Rillieux, Henry Boyd, and George Peake developed useful and important inventions that improved the lives of people of all races across America and beyond. They stood as counterexamples to the dominant idea that African Americans were inferior to whites. Though they could not erase the prejudice that most white Americans felt toward blacks, their inventions challenged it. In doing so, they paved the way for greater acceptance of black inventors and inventions in the future.

CHAPTER TWO
MECHANICAL EXPERIMENTATION AND THE INDUSTRIAL REVOLUTION

Ever since the first European settlers arrived on what would become American soil, it had been a land dominated by agricultural production. The 13 original colonies were largely rural, and farming operations occupied huge patches of land. Though cities were developed as the years went on, there were no real centers of manufacturing production in the entire country. The outbreak of the Civil War in the mid-1800s and the postslavery period immediately following its conclusion were a time of massive changes to the United States. This was true both socially, as African Americans were finally being integrated into society as free men and women, and economically. Since free farming labor was now unavailable, other areas of industry needed to adapt to fill the country's economic needs.

With improved technology, such as steamboats, trains, and the telegram, came improved manufacturing procedures. The downfall of slavery gave way to the rise of industry. This was the time of the Industrial Revolution.

Historians point to the abolition of slavery as the biggest cause of the Industrial Revolution, but there were many other factors that caused the explosion of manufacturing. Not only did formerly enslaved African Americans increase the size of the workforce, but the United States also experienced a huge spike in immigration during the postwar years. Because of the availability of large numbers of laborers, it was easier for businesses to access natural resources, such as iron, coal, and natural gas. As a result, a fresh generation of inventors, both black and white, had new materials to work with. There were massive improvements made in nearly every area of industry during this time period, brought along by endless experimentation and relentless innovations. Historians Allan Nevins and Henry Steele Commager wrote, "Americans probably patented more numerous and more [genius] inventions [during these years] than any other people."[12] From 1860 to 1900, the federal government issued more than 650,000 unique patents.

Though not all of these inventions were powerful enough to shape the world, many of them were. One of the most famous inventors of the time, Alexander Graham Bell, developed the telephone, which was patented in 1876. Thomas Edison, the father of electricity, was producing new innovations and acquiring new patents during this time. Moreover, black inventors were allowed much more freedom during these years, and the number of unique and effective inventions created by African Americans highlights that fact.

Alexander Graham Bell's telephone was one of the greatest technological improvements in human history. African American inventors were inspired by such an incredible feat of engineering.

Their contributions were crucial to the rapid success and spread of the Industrial Revolution, even if they were not always making the newspaper headlines.

Leading Minds Laying Rails

Black inventors of this period were talented workers with machinery of all kinds. In general, however, their area of specialization was on the nation's numerous railroads. Many of the most notable African American inventors of the Industrial Revolution created devices and modifications that made train travel easier, cheaper, safer, and more comfortable. Their railway expertise was not the result of mere coincidence. American railroad companies hired thousands of black workers, mostly as general, unskilled laborers. Their hard work allowed countless miles of train tracks all across the country to be completed. However, most of these employees were only hired for their ability to swing a hammer. Even after the Civil War, there was widespread racial discrimination, and few companies were interested in the intellect of black workers. Over time, many of these black employees became familiar with the workings of trains. Because they were so heavily involved with their production, they knew which railroad technologies needed improvement. The most innovative of them took on the challenges of making these improvements.

In truth, the railroads of this time were in need of improvement. The trains of the mid-1800s were slow, unreliable, dangerous, and generally uncomfortable. That was a problem for all Americans, whether they rode as passengers on trains or not. Effective transportation was a major contributing factor to the country's continued economic growth. A fast and efficient railroad system would allow companies to transport raw materials to factories for manufacturing and the finished products to consumers all across the nation. As rails began to expand to cover huge cities and small towns, more and more people, both black and white, were interested in improving them.

One of the most successful of these train-related inventions was a direct improvement to an extremely dangerous part of railroad work: connecting the cars of a train. This process was called coupling, and in the 1870s and 1880s, it was done completely by hand. Each car had a piece of metal—called a coupler—sticking out of its front and back ends. At the time, these couplers were U-shaped hooks. Workers would

Black railway workers were employed to do the hard labor required to lay down tracks. Because many African Americans worked closely with the railroads, they were able to change rail travel.

slowly back one car up to another, trying to align the two couplers perfectly. At just the right moment, someone had to insert a strong metal pin between the couplers; this pin kept the cars from separating. Accomplishing this task required perfect timing. Workers who tried to insert the pin a second too late risked being crushed between the cars. Many railroad workers lost arms and legs in exactly this way, and some even died. A contemporary poet wrote:

Suddenly there comes a messenger;
God have mercy hear them pray;
As they hear the fearful story—
Killed while coupling cars today.[13]

The most obvious solution to this problem was to develop a machine that would join cars automatically, and many inventors tried to do just that. One of these was an African American railroad worker named Andrew Jackson Beard. Born in 1849 as a slave, as an adult,

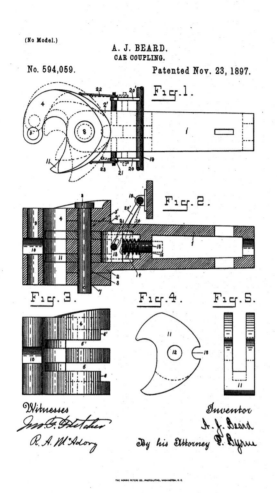

Andrew Jackson Beard's coupling device, shown here, improved railroad safety conditions and saved lives.

accident. In the 1890s, he began working on a way to fix the problem. After months of diligent work, he built an automatic coupler that could join railroad cars both quickly and safely. Explaining the mechanism of his invention, he wrote, "Horizontal jaws engage each other to connect the cars."[14] Beard patented the device in 1897, and it was called the Jenny Coupler.

Seeing an opportunity to make and market Beard's invention, a group of businessmen paid him $50,000 for the rights to his patent. Today, that amount is roughly equivalent to $1.5 million.

Beard worked at an Alabama railroad yard after his emancipation. It was there that he witnessed the dangers of coupling cars firsthand. It was reported that he lost one of his legs in a car coupling

A Breath of Fresh Air

Humphrey H. Reynolds was another

AMERICA BECOMES
AN INDUSTRIAL POWER

Even after more than a century, the effect of the Industrial Revolution on the United States is easy to see. In the 1820s, about 90 percent of Americans lived in rural areas. Even the few people who lived in cities and towns often earned their living making agricultural tools or buying, selling, and shipping farming products. By 1890, right in the middle of the Industrial Revolution, one-third of all Americans lived in cities. More and more of the city dwellers, in addition, worked in manufacturing or had commercial jobs that did not focus on agricultural trade.

The transportation system underwent similarly huge changes during this time. As late as 1840, the country had less than 3,000 miles (4,800 km) of railroad track. Those who wanted to travel long distances had to take ships or make a long and difficult journey in a stagecoach or wagon. The rise of the railroad, even with its flaws, made these older forms of travel obsolete. In 1880, roughly 90,000 miles (144,000 km) of track ran through the United States.

Despite the general improvement to the American quality of life, the changes that happened during this time were not always positive. Factories pumped pollution into the air; trains were dirty; and workers were underpaid and labored long hours, often in terrible conditions. Many disliked the increasing speed of an industrial society and the growing emphasis on material goods. They urged a return to the quieter and slower pace of rural life. However, once the Industrial Revolution was set in motion, it was impossible to derail.

African American railroad worker who set out to solve a problem by inventing something new. Reynolds was an employee of the Pullman Company, a very large and successful business best known for manufacturing passenger cars for trains. He worked as a porter, and his main job was to make sure the train's passengers were attended to.

Unfortunately, train travel at the time was far from comfortable. With the windows shut, the interior of a train car generally grew hot and stuffy. Frequently, travelers would ask Reynolds to open their windows. Trains, however, were notorious for kicking up huge clouds of dust and smoke, so having the windows open was generally not a good way to

The emergence of factories, such as this one, was both good and bad. Middle-class Americans were able to get better goods more cheaply, but poorer people had to work long, hard hours to produce them.

get fresh air. It seemed impossible to find a comfortable balance between the two extremes.

Like Andrew Jackson Beard, Reynolds had a mind that was always questioning. He worked on the problem during his spare time and eventually developed a device that he called a ventilator. The ventilator filtered out the worst of the smoke and grime that rushed in through the open train windows, allowing passengers to enjoy the benefits of the outside air without choking on it. Reynolds's new invention was so impressive that the head of the Pullman Company himself wanted to see it in action. After recognizing the immense benefits of such a ventilator, he arranged to have ventilators installed on every car Pullman produced. However, the head of the company did not want to pay Reynolds for his hard work. Regardless, Reynolds's invention received plenty of notice, and a great deal of approval as well. One news article referred to it as "the ingenious folding-window ventilator in use on all Pullman cars."[15]

Though the corporation's strategy of ignoring Reynolds might have worked against many black inventors, Reynolds was not willing to back down. Few African Americans of the time would have dared go up against a wealthy and powerful corporation. Reynolds, however, successfully argued for his rights to his invention. A contemporary journalist wrote, "He got out of the service of the Pullmans, sued them, and got a verdict for ten thousand dollars."[16]

The Real McCoy

Many other black inventors devised improvements to rail travel as well, though most did not benefit from these creations financially. In 1890, for example, an inventor named Philip Downing received a patent for an electrical train switch. This new technology would allow rail companies to regulate the distribution of power to their trains. Landrow Bell patented an improvement

to train smokestacks in 1871. The hot sparks and cinders from 19th-century smokestacks could ignite anything next to the rails and cause dangerous fires; his new design prevented that. A.B. Blackburn developed a new type of railroad signal in 1888. This improved the general safety of railway travel. Many of these inventions, just like those of Beard and Reynolds, greatly improved the railroad industry.

These inventors were important, but a man named Elijah McCoy made the most significant contributions of any African American to railroads. McCoy was born in 1844, the son of two slaves who were able to escape to Ontario, Canada. His family lived there for three years after his birth before moving back to America, finding a home in Ypsilanti, Michigan, in 1847. Even as a young boy, he was fascinated by machinery. As a teenager, he spent several years in Scotland, where he studied mechanical engineering. Around 1865, when the Civil War was coming to an end, McCoy returned to Michigan and began looking for a job as an engineer. As was the case for many intelligent African Americans, racial prejudice prevented him from getting a position that met his talents. No matter how competent, creative, and intelligent McCoy was, the white employers of Michigan were not ready to hire a black man to fill an engineering post.

McCoy eventually took a job for which he was overqualified: a fireman on the Michigan Central Railroad. In the 1800s, a train's fireman was primarily responsible for shoveling coal into the train's engine, where it was burned for fuel, and oiling the engine to make it run at maximum efficiency. Though the first of these tasks was physically challenging, the second took more time to accomplish. Train engines were made up of dozens of parts, and nearly all of them were made of metal. When the train ran, these pieces rubbed against each other. Over time, this would wear them down. The constant rubbing also made the engine extremely hot. To make the parts last longer and to reduce the risk of fire, the engine had to be covered in a lubricant approximately every two hours. This lubricant cooled the engine and coated the metal parts, protecting them from wear. The train, however, could not run while the fireman was oiling the engine. As a result, trains rarely ran for more than two hours at a time. This became a major area of concern, especially on longer trips.

This modern picture of a steam locomotive shows how complex their engine systems are. Keeping them up and running was a difficult task.

A Revolutionary Cup

Elijah McCoy believed he could devise a more efficient method of lubricating engines. He was even confident that his new system could eliminate the need for frequent oil stops. He thought up possible solutions while he was on the job, and after leaving work for the day, he ran experiments to test his ideas in his workshop at home. In the early 1870s, after many failures and mistakes, he created a system that worked. McCoy's method was based on a drip cup, which was a container that held oil and released it into the engine at a slow and steady rate. That made it possible to lubricate the engine automatically. The best part was that the drip cup worked even when the engine was in operation. Thanks to McCoy's automatic lubricator, trains were now able to travel many miles without stopping. This accelerated rail traffic and saved both travelers and merchants a lot of time and money.

McCoy took out a patent on his lubrication system in 1872. The invention, he wrote, "provides for the continuous flow of oil on the gears and other moving parts of a machine in order to keep it lubricated properly and continuously and thereby do away with the necessity of shutting down the machine periodically."[17] Railroad officials who studied the device saw its value and were quick to install it on their own trains. Even the most prejudiced of railway operators recognized that they could not afford to continue with the old method when McCoy's new device was so much more effective. Before long, nearly all American railroads used some version of McCoy's invention.

McCoy continued to invent throughout his life. Over the next few years he developed several improvements to his original lubricating system and patented these as well. Later, he designed drip cup lubrication techniques for use in other kinds of engines. By the time he died in 1929, he had taken out patents for inventions of all kinds, and his career had made him a minor celebrity—even outside the black community. In 1926, one journalist wrote, "Elijah McCoy, a Negro inventor [has been issued] fifty-seven patents in the United States and ten in Europe. The universally used lubricating cup for machinery is one of his inventions and later ideas of his are receiving serious consideration in the laboratories of the country."[18]

A Shoemaker from Suriname

Although many African American

THE FAKE MCCOY

Today, the expression "the real McCoy" is often used to mean "the real thing, not a copy." Some books that discuss Elijah McCoy's life and work claim that he was the original "McCoy" from this phrase. The historical legend is that others imitated many of McCoy's inventions, but the imitations were not as good as McCoy's original products. Tired of these poor copies, railroad officials began demanding "the real McCoy"—that is, the product manufactured by McCoy himself. The phrase soon moved into use in regular conversation and developed the more general meaning it carries today.

However, most experts who study the origins of words and phrases reject this theory. The phrase "the real McKay" was being used in Scotland when Elijah McCoy was still a boy, and "the real McCoy" is most likely an American variation of this term. Moreover, McCoy's inventions do not seem to have much to do with the popularity of the phrase in the United States. "The real McCoy" appears for the first time in print in 1908, long after McCoy patented his best-known inventions, and no early mentions of the phrase directly refer to Elijah McCoy and his works. Though it is a remarkable coincidence, it is unlikely that the phrase has any relationship to the great African American inventor.

inventors made names for themselves in railroads, there were also other industries where black innovators stood out. William A. Lavalette of Washington, D.C., for instance, patented two improvements for printing presses in 1878. One year later, Thomas Elkins earned a patent for an early method of refrigeration. Joseph Lee of Massachusetts developed two machines in the late 1800s: one that could speed up the process of bread making and one that could automatically reduce stale loaves of bread to crumbs. Joseph Dickinson, an organ builder by trade, established his own organ factory and held patents on several organ designs. He was even commissioned to craft an organ for the royal family of Portugal.

One of the greatest black inventors of the Industrial Revolution was a man named Jan Ernst Matzeliger. Matzeliger was born in 1852 in Suriname, a Dutch colony on the northern coast of South America. Like Elijah McCoy, Matzeliger's interest in mechanics started young. He also showed that he had great talent for math and engineering. When he was just 10 years old, he became an apprentice in a Suriname machine shop. Despite this opportunity to start a career, Matzeliger also had a desire to see the world. When he was 19, he joined the crew of a merchant ship. A year or two later, his ship made a stop in Philadelphia, Pennsylvania, and Matzeliger decided to abandon a life on the seas and make a new home in the United States.

However, Matzeliger's time in Philadelphia was brief. Like McCoy, when people saw the color of his skin, they were unwilling to give him the job that he deserved. Though racial prejudice was the main issue, Matzeliger's poor English probably also played a role in keeping him from a good job. Before long, he moved to Boston and then to the nearby city of Lynn, Massachusetts, which was known for its booming shoe industry. For a time, he worked at a shoe factory. The work was dull, repetitive, and unsatisfying, but it did allow him to make some kind of living. To make himself more employable, Matzeliger studied English and physics at night. Even so, he simply could not find a better job.

Jan Matzeliger's career got off to a bad start, but his innovative designs would eventually revolutionize the entire shoemaking industry.

The Science of Shoemaking

Because Matzeliger's job at the shoe factory was repetitive and did not require him to apply his intelligence, he was able to turn his attention to other things, even as he worked. He began analyzing the process by which the shoes were made. For almost all of history, shoes had been created by professional shoemakers. These were craftsmen who produced one pair of shoes at a time, commonly made for the unique foot of a specific customer. In the 1870s, however, the factory in Lynn did things differently. It used a system in which shoes would pass through several different work stations; this was called an assembly line. At one station, a worker cut out soles; at another, workers would sew parts of each shoe together. On most parts of the line, the workers had machines that helped them do those jobs. Compared to the methods of a traditional shoemaker, this procedure sped up the manufacturing process, making shoes less expensive and more widely available.

The assembly line method had its own problems, however. One important step in 19th-century shoe manufacturing was known as lasting. This term comes from the necessary process of making a last, which is a mold that takes the shape of a customer's foot. The upper part of the shoe was formed around this mold, and then attached to the thick sole. Lasting is the process of attaching the last to the sole. In the early 1870s, the lasting process was carried out exclusively by hand. The workers who did this job were called lasters. Lasting was delicate work that required a trained, skilled, and steady hand. There were no lasting machines, and most shoemakers believed that such a machine could not exist. A laster at that time claimed, "No man can build a machine that will last shoes and take away the job of the laster, unless he [can] make a machine that has fingers like a laster—and that is impossible."[19]

Because there was no effective lasting machine, the entire process of producing a shoe was slowed down considerably. Though machines were used for other parts of the shoe, the process of lasting was still done by hand and took a much longer time. As a result, factories could not supply enough shoes to meet consumer demand. That kept profits low, prices high, and workers unhappy, since their pay was based on the number of shoes the factory produced. As a factory worker himself, Matzeliger recognized the problem. However, he did not share the standard view that the lasting process could never be

This image shows traditional lasting tools alongside a standard last. In the 19th century, lasters had to go through a long process to finish most shoes.

automated. At some point in the late 1870s, he began to try to construct a lasting machine of his own.

An Intricate Design

For Matzeliger, the design process was slow, challenging, and frustrating. Because he had no money to buy equipment, he had to build models out of materials that he could obtain for little or no cost. He tried many designs and new ideas, but he seemed to be no closer to success after several years. It was not until 1880 that Matzeliger's hard work and persistence finally paid off. Using wires, wood, and an old cigar box, he put together a crude model of an automated lasting machine. Though his device could not actually last shoes (a functional model would have required much more expensive parts), Matzeliger was certain that his design would prove effective once it was built.

His next step was to try to patent the invention. To do that, Matzeliger had to construct the actual machine, and that meant finding the money to buy the materials he needed. He worked out a deal with two investors. In exchange for money to build a working model of his device, Matzeliger promised to give the investors a portion of whatever his profits were once he sold it. In the 1880s, and even today, this is a common method of raising funds for a potential invention. While Matzeliger would give up some of his future profits, the deal allowed him to make his dream machine a reality. Without a working model, he could not be issued a patent, and without a patent, he could not earn anything from the machine at all.

Matzeliger soon completed his model and submitted his design to the patent office. The machine was extremely complex; one historian wrote that his patent application consisted of "seven pages of complicated drawings and eight pages of printed material specifying how his invention worked."[20] Even with such extensive paperwork, the patent officers were initially unable to figure out the workings of the machine. The federal government sent the

(No Model.) J. E. MATZELIGER. 7 Sheets—Sheet 2.
LASTING MACHINE.
No. 274,207. Patented Mar. 20, 1883.

Jan Matzeliger's famous machine for the automated lasting of shoes, shown here, was incredibly complicated. Once the machines were built, he was able to change the shoe industry forever.

MAKING SHOES AFFORDABLE

When people first witnessed Matzeliger's incredible invention in 1885, they were shocked. His process would eventually save shoe companies so much time that they would be able to reduce their prices significantly—leading to the widespread affordability of shoes. One historian described the process:

[The machine's] main working component was a single pincers resembling an ordinary pair of pliers with the jaws thinned and bent. A worker placed an insole and an upper on a last and positioned the last on the machine. The machine drove a tack, turned the shoe, pleated the leather, drove another tack, and continued until the shoe was finished, exactly reproducing the technique used by hand lasters. The job took one minute.

Those who saw it could hardly believe their eyes. Working five times faster than a human worker, the device perfectly [made] 75 difficult pairs of women's shoes. Other machines had performed parts of these operations; this was the first to combine so many complex steps and produce shoes indistinguishable from handmade ones. And it could handle all shoe styles and any grade of leather.[1]

1. Dennis Karwatka, "Shoe Laster," *American Heritage's Invention & Technology*, Fall 2010. inventionandtech.com/content/shoe-laster.

officers to Lynn, where Matzeliger had to give them a demonstration before they would issue the patent. At last, in 1883, Matzeliger received the patent he had worked so hard to achieve. Over the next two years, he added improvements to make his lasting machine more durable and more effective. The patenting of his machine marked a major turning point in the history of shoe production, both in America and worldwide.

Changing an Entire Industry

Jan Matzeliger's invention was an

immediate success. By introducing his machine and replacing the slower hand lasters, factories were able to turn out as many as 700 pairs of shoes a day. At best, the previous average was about 50 pairs per day. In addition, the cost of producing a pair of shoes was halved; as a result, millions of people who never thought they could afford a good pair of shoes were able to buy shoes for their entire family. With such huge profits, most shoe companies were able to significantly increase the wages for their workers. In fact, the only people who were unhappy with Matzeliger's invention were the lasters. They tried to minimize the damage by arguing that an automated machine only increased the need for skilled laborers. "The machine must be operated by an expert laster," one worker claimed, "otherwise the machine is of no effect. The machine is virtually only an assistant to the laster."[21] Regardless of this argument, lasters began to disappear completely from the industry. Their way of doing things had suddenly become outdated.

Matzeliger did not live long after finally seeing his machine succeed. In 1886, he contracted the deadly disease tuberculosis. Three years later, at the young age of 37, he was dead. Despite his untimely sickness, Matzeliger was an important figure in the history of American industry. By creating his lasting machine, he accomplished something that most people thought was impossible. His genius completely changed the way shoes were manufactured. Historian Portia P. James wrote, "Not many individual inventors would be able to influence, much less revolutionize, a whole industry."[22] Matzeliger was one of the few who could—and did. Workers in shoe factories around the world owed him a debt of gratitude. He improved their lives—and the lives of everyone who needed a pair of shoes.

Slow but Steady Progress

The black inventors of the post-Civil War years did not have an easy path. Racial prejudice prevented Elijah McCoy and Jan Ernst Matzeliger from finding work that used their exceptional minds to the fullest. The Pullman Company tried to take advantage of Humphrey Reynolds's ventilator. Inventors such as Andrew Jackson Beard spent a large portion of their lives laboring at dangerous and unappealing railroad or factory jobs. Just as it was before the abolition of slavery, there is no way of knowing if African Americans of the period had invention ideas stolen from them.

Still, black inventors during the Industrial Revolution fared better than their predecessors. American society after the Civil War prized inventiveness and ingenuity, and though there was still a lot of racial tension in America, great inventors created a path to success for black Americans who had those traits. As the years progressed, white Americans seemed increasingly willing to judge an invention by its use, rather than by the race of the person who had invented it. Moreover, it was easier for the African American mechanics and tinkerers of the late 1800s to obtain patents than it had been for equally impressive innovators, such as Henry Boyd, just a few decades before. By 1900, black inventors were still far from the mainstream, but with each impressive invention created by an African American, respect for their ideas increased.

CHAPTER THREE
ELECTRIC AMERICA

In addition to the incredible achievements by black inventors in the late 1800s, inventors of other races were working equally hard to advance American technology. Thomas Edison made the use of electricity widespread, providing reliable light for millions of Americans. Alexander Graham Bell developed and refined new technology to allow for instantaneous communication across long distances—the first telephone. The first movies, originally called moving pictures, were entering production, and would eventually become a cultural staple throughout the world. When the inventions from all races are combined, it is easy to see how the world of the early 1900s was a completely different place from what it had been just 50 years before. People were seeing and doing things that exceeded anyone's wildest imagination.

The common link between many innovations of the late 19th century is the increased use of electricity. Electric power was at the front of many of these great inventors' minds. Without it, Bell would not have been able to develop the telephone, Edison's light bulbs would not have made it out of his sketchbook, and movies would be nothing more than a dream. Hundreds of other inventors during this time would not have been inspired to make new and exciting products if not for the groundbreaking use of electricity in the United States. Historians call the period of the late 1800s to the early 1900s the Age of Electricity.

Thomas Edison is considered, even today, one of the greatest inventive minds to ever live. He is undoubtedly the most famous innovator to emerge from the Age of Electricity that he helped begin. However, he was far from the only person who harnessed the power of electric currents to do great things. Others included Granville T. Woods and Lewis Latimer, both of whom were African American. Though they are not as recognizable as Edison, these two men performed amazing feats of engineering and creativity in the name of invention.

A Brief History of Electricity

Although it became widespread in the late 1800s, electricity was not a new discovery at that time. People had been aware of this type of power for a long time. For example, people were familiar with static electricity for centuries. Lightning, another natural form of electricity, was known to ancient societies as well. Some cultures that caught fish were often familiar with electric eels and other marine creatures that carry an electric charge. However, none of these people had any real understanding of what electricity was, how it worked, or how humans could use it.

During the 1600s and 1700s, Western scientists started to study electrical energy with a new

Benjamin Franklin, one of America's Founding Fathers, was also one of the first people to do breakthrough experiments with natural electricity.

understanding. Through the work of famed researchers such as Benjamin Franklin, a human understanding of electricity gradually formed. Franklin and other scientists ran important experiments that led scientists to comprehend the properties of electricity, the relationship between electricity and magnetism, and the electrical system in the human body. Still, most scientists explored electricity in theory—few were interested in harnessing electrical energy for practical applications. Well into the 1800s, electricity was viewed more as a scientific oddity than as a force that people might be able to utilize for themselves.

In the absence of electric power, Americans of the time used a variety of fuels. To light their homes, people commonly used oil lamps. (The whale oil industry was massive in early America, and a great deal was obtained by whalers using Lewis Temple's toggle harpoon.) Factories were often built near waterfalls to take advantage of the power generated by moving water. Farmers occasionally used windmills to harness the force of the wind. One of the most popular fuels of the period was natural gas. It was easy to burn, and it produced a steady, reliable light suitable for both indoor use and streetlamps. To

the people of the 1860s, one historian wrote, "gas was such a clean, efficient, inexpensive source of lighting that it seemed improbable that any other mode of illumination would, or could, replace the gaslamp."[23]

Still, a few innovative scientists saw electricity's potential as a substitute for gas. In 1807, British scientist Humphry Davy built a primitive version of an electric light bulb. Though the bulb had little practical value, Davy's success got other researchers interested in that concept. Over the following decades, a steadily growing number of scientists and technicians worked on the problem of developing a safe and reliable electric light. Though they did not know if electric light could ever be an effective substitute for gas, they were determined to find out. They made progress, but it was slow. Many scientists built on each other's work and moved gradually toward the construction of a reliable and efficient electric light.

The most important breakthrough came in the late 1870s. After many months of research, Thomas Edison had found a way to build a bulb that gave off plenty of light, lasted for hours, and was relatively inexpensive both to buy and to run. The design was not totally his own; other inventors had come up with some of these ideas

Gas lamps, such as the one shown here, were the most popular form of lighting for many years—until the revolutionary light bulb.

elements in a light bulb of his own invention at roughly the same time. Nonetheless, Edison was the first American to put all these ideas together and demonstrate that an effective electric light bulb could be a reality. Still, electric light was slow to catch on among the public. Scientists and inventors across America, however, saw that a new age was dawning. Electricity, they realized, was the power of the future.

Sailor to Office Boy

Among the first Americans to recognize the potential of electricity was a black man named Lewis Latimer. He was born in Massachusetts in 1848, the son of two escaped slaves. During the Civil War, Latimer served in the U.S. Navy. Because he would have been too long before he began researching electric light, and an English inventor used many of the same design young to enlist, he lied about his age and entered service when he was just 16. When the war was over, Latimer returned to Massachusetts and was able to get a job with a law firm that specialized in patents and inventions. At first, he worked as an office assistant, delivering messages and doing other simple tasks. His youth and inexperience made him a perfect fit for these simple jobs. However, it is also likely that Latimer's race kept him from being considered for positions that carried more authority, no matter how well he performed his current job.

Latimer did not wish to remain an office assistant for long. He was soon intrigued by the work of the company's draftsmen. Draftsmen

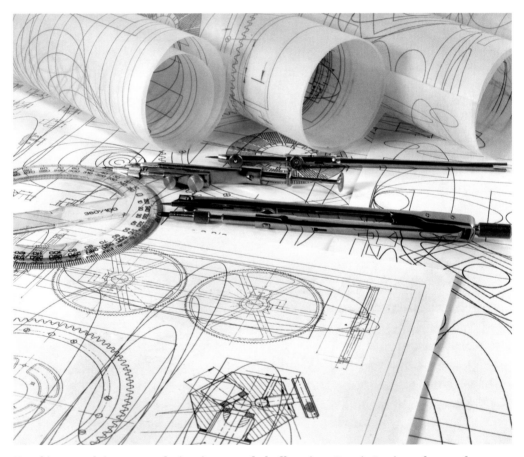

Drafting work is extremely intricate and challenging. Lewis Latimer learned a lot of things about electricity and mechanical engineering through his work as a draftsman.

ARTIST
AND INVENTOR

Lewis Latimer was a well-rounded man. In addition to his remarkable scientific abilities, he was a fine musician, a volunteer teacher of English to immigrants, and even a poet. Later in his life, he published a small book of his poems. Many of the poems in the book were love poems; others were Latimer's poetic thoughts on life, death, and the world around him:

What is there, in this world, besides your loves
To keep us here?
Ambition's course is paved with hopes deterred,
With doubt and fear.
Wealth brings no joy,
And brazen-throated fame,
Leaves us at last
Nought but an empty urn.
Oh soul, receive the truth
E're heaven sends thy recall
Nought here deserves one thought but love,
For love is all.[1]

1. Quoted in Charles R. Brooks, "Black Inventor Helped Develop Telephone, Electric Lighting," *The News* (Frederick, MD), February 10, 1971.

are artists who specialize in drawing machines and blueprints. To apply for a patent, inventors had to provide intricate and precise pictures that showed every detail of their inventions. Because few inventors had enough artistic skill to draft these pictures on their own, patent lawyers typically had expert draftsmen on staff to create the diagrams. Latimer wanted to learn everything he could about drafting. He studied specific drawing techniques at home and practiced them whenever he could. Before long, his supervisors recognized his talent, and he was promoted to the post of draftsman. By 1875, he was the head draftsman for the firm. A journalist later wrote that Latimer had been "thrust upward by his singular [impressive] talent and drive."[24]

As an employee at a law firm specializing in inventions, Latimer's work as a draftsman brought him into contact with many inventors. The most famous of these was Alexander Graham Bell, the inventor of the telephone. Latimer was actually the artist behind several drawings that helped Bell claim the patents he applied for. To draw these designs as accurately as possible, Latimer pushed himself to learn as much as he could about Bell's work. In the process, Latimer became interested in the principles of electricity that drove the innovation of Bell's project. As Latimer read more and more about electricity as a power source, he was eventually convinced that this form of energy could help Americans in new and important ways.

Maxim and Latimer

In the late 1870s, Latimer began looking for a job that would give him time to pursue his interest—and talent—in technology. After moving to Bridgeport, Connecticut, in 1880, he was offered a position at the United States Electric Light Company. The head engineer of the company was a man named Hiram Maxim, an inventor who was already renowned among scientists for his work with electric power. Though Thomas Edison had already patented the first effective electric light bulb, Maxim believed he could improve on Edison's design. The biggest problem of Edison's original bulbs was that they did not last very long. Maxim thought he could drastically increase their life span. To accomplish that, he hired the most intelligent and hardworking people he could find. One of these people was Lewis Latimer.

Maxim and Latimer identified what they thought would be the best way to improve the longevity of the light bulb: remaking its filament. In a light bulb, the filament is the thin, wire-like object in the middle of the bulb, and it is the part that gives off light. Designing a filament was the focus of Latimer's first few months in Maxim's employ. In 1881, just a year after joining Maxim's firm, Latimer patented a new and more efficient way of making filaments. His patent application described this improvement as "a continuous strip of carbon secured to metallic wires."[25] The upgraded procedure resulted in light bulbs that were better and

Hiram Maxim, a renowned inventor in the early 20th century, was a key figure in getting Lewis Latimer noticed by the scientific community.

cheaper than what Edison had been able to develop. During his time at the United States Electric Light Company, Latimer was issued several patents, each of which was directly responsible for improving the widespread use of electric lighting.

However, Latimer did not spend all of his time inventing. His work had made him a respected authority on electric lighting, and Maxim gave him more and more responsibility. He was sent to oversee factory operations in Philadelphia and other U.S. cities. Latimer also traveled to England to set up a new factory and to Montreal, Quebec, to guide workers in installing electric lights in train stations. In Montreal, he even learned some French so he could communicate with employees who spoke little or no English.

THE STRUGGLE OF A FEMALE INVENTOR

As difficult as it was for African American men to patent inventions during the 1800s, earning a patent was even harder for a woman. Not only were 19th-century women encouraged to stay out of public life, but most people also believed that women were incapable of understanding science and technology. Few people believed that women could be inventors. The most famous African American woman to receive a patent at that time did so in 1928, when Marjorie Joyner patented a permanent wave machine to curl or straighten hair.

However, a few other black women had success before this period. In 1884, a woman named Judy W. Reed patented a device for kneading and rolling bread dough. A year later, Sarah E. Goode was issued a patent for what was called a cabinet bed, which combined a bed and a writing desk in a single piece of furniture. Though little documentation has survived about either Reed or Goode, many historians believe that they were both African American. The first black woman to patent an invention was most likely one of these two women.

Years later, Latimer wrote about his time in Montreal: "My day was spent climbing telegraph poles and locating [electric] lamps on them with the assistance of my laborers who seemed much impressed with my effort to speak their language."[26]

Electrical Expertise

Latimer's boss, Hiram Maxim, was a successful businessman, a talented scientist, and a skilled inventor. However, he was not well liked by his peers. In 1880, one of Thomas Edison's assistants wrote, "I did not like Maxim and was distrustful of him. Several times he had the [nerve] to claim to others [right in front of me] ideas given [to] him by me."[27] Despite the great opportunities he had been given, Latimer left Maxim's company after only a few years. He worked for several other firms before being offered a new job as a draftsman—this time with Maxim's greatest rival, Thomas Edison.

Over the next 12 years, Latimer held a variety of positions within Edison's Electric Light Company (known today as General Electric).

One of his main tasks was to work with the firm's legal department. In the growing and increasingly valuable world of electric light, inventors and manufacturers regularly filed lawsuits against each other for patent infringement. Latimer helped Edison both defend his patents against lawsuits from other inventors and assisted in filing claims against those who unfairly made use of Edison's work. That required Latimer to make a thorough study of each electric device in question. In the late 1880s, Latimer's knowledge of electric lighting was greater than almost anyone else's.

In 1890, he wrote a book titled *Incandescent Electric Lighting: A Practical Description of the Edison System*, which, for many years, was the definitive work on the subject.

By 1896, Latimer was highly regarded as a technical and practical expert in the fields of electric lighting and patent law. Two of the biggest electric companies in the United States (General Electric and Westinghouse) had established a special governing body to oversee patent disputes outside of the court system, and Latimer was chosen to work for this elite group. Fifteen years later, Latimer left this position

The Edison Pioneers, shown here in a group photo, were some of the most important innovators and creators of their era.

and became an independent patent consultant. During these years, he also patented several new devices, among them a new type of elevator and a mechanism to cool and disinfect air. When he died in 1928, he was mourned as a fine colleague and a brilliant inventor.

Lewis Latimer was a member of a group of electricians, inventors, and scientists who had been involved with Thomas Edison. They named themselves the Edison Pioneers, and after he died, they wrote: "We rejoice in the pleasant memory of having been associated with him in a great accomplishment for all peoples."[28]

The Genius from Columbus

Granville T. Woods was also an African American inventor with a particular interest in electricity and electrical devices. Woods was born shortly before the Civil War, in 1856. Like many scientists who worked with electricity in the 19th century, Woods's life was connected to the life and work of Thomas Edison. In fact, Woods was often called "the black Edison." Woods was able to make a long, successful career for himself despite little formal education and the realities of racism in America in the late 19th century.

Not much is known about Woods's early life. He was born in Columbus, Ohio, on April 23, 1856, to free black parents. He only attended school for a few years before dropping out and spending his time working. As a teenager, Woods held a variety of jobs, including stints as a laborer in a steel mill, a railroad worker, and an apprentice in a machine shop. Woods's passion, however, was electrical engineering. Woods read and studied the subject relentlessly. Like many other black inventors, however, he had difficulty finding work that matched his skills. In the 1880s, after years of frustration, Woods decided to take his life in a new direction. Since he could not find an employer who would give him the work he wanted to do, he went into business for himself instead. Opening a workshop in Cincinnati, he immediately started inventing.

Starting his own business was a wise move in many ways, because Woods had an exceptionally innovative mind. He was incredibly versatile, too. Where Latimer's inventions were mainly related to electric lighting and Elijah McCoy largely focused on engines and oiling systems, Woods developed a wide range of devices. One of his first patents, for example, was for

Known across America as a great creator, Granville T. Woods was an incredible inventor. His work produced significant safety improvements to the rail industry.

particular expertise, and that was electricity. A few months after founding his new company, Woods patented a new kind of transmitter for telephones. The following year, he was issued a patent for a device that he called a "telegraphony." This invention combined two of the greatest innovations in communication the world had ever seen—the telephone and the telegraph. The telegraph, invented before the Civil War, allowed messages to be sent through wires using a system of long and short electrical impulses. In telegraphs, different combinations of impulses stood for different letters, which would be interpreted by a telegraph operator. Woods's innovation was to add telephone technology to the telegraph system, allowing senders to choose either their voices or standard telegraph codes to send their messages.

improvements to a steam engine, and one of his most famous inventions was an air brake to improve the stopping ability of trains. He even owned a patent for an egg incubator that was capable of hatching hundreds of eggs at a time.

Still, Woods had an area of

In 1887, Woods perfected an even more important invention.

ALTERNATIVE LOCOMOTION

Several years before a system called the third rail came into general use as a way to propel trains with electricity, Granville T. Woods patented a different method that relied on a similar design. In 1893, the *New York Times* published a brief article about his invention under the headline "May Drive Out the Trolley," which read,

> *There was a very interesting and remarkable test to-day on the short section of railroad here [New York City], where the system of underground conduits for electric propulsion invented by Granville T. Woods, the colored electrician of Brooklyn and Cincinnati, is being experimented with. The system consists of a conduit [a long channel or tube], in which are placed at regular intervals ... watertight boxes, from which project contact points at each side of the slot. These contact points form a connection with a long shoe which is fastened on the bottom of the [train] car and runs in the slot.*[1]

The experiment demonstrated that the device could work even in bad weather. According to the reporter, Woods's invention was a clear improvement over the overhead wires that powered trolleys. Other observers agreed. The article quoted a railway worker as saying, "The day of the trolley is past. I would rather own this patent than any other for electric street-car propulsion in the world."[2]

1. Quoted in "May Drive Out the Trolley," *New York Times*, September 16, 1893.

2. Quoted in "May Drive Out the Trolley," *New York Times*.

For years, telegraph wires could commonly be found alongside railroad tracks. These wires carried messages to and from stationmasters at various stops along the rail route. However, it was not possible to telegraph a message between a station and a moving train, or between two moving trains. A way to quickly and easily contact conductors on a train had yet to be invented. Because the moving train had no outside communication, it was impossible for it to know if something unexpected was blocking its path. Rails could be flooded or something could be stuck on the rails ahead, and those on the train would have no way of knowing. That isolation created potentially dangerous situations. Several inventors had tried to build devices that would allow trains to communicate while they were in transit. None had succeeded, however, until Woods.

Woods's device, called the synchronous multiplex railway telegraph, allowed trains to tap into the telegraph wires along the tracks as they sped along so they could send and receive messages. "A circuit of wire extends along the track," Woods wrote, "and another circuit is carried by the [train] car."[29] It was now possible for engineers and stationmasters to send messages back and forth, even while a train was already on its route. Woods had helped make rail travel much safer—and he was just getting started.

Still Not Satisfied

Woods followed this invention, which had already changed the entire world of rail travel, with even more, including a safety circuit to cut down on electrical fires and a grooved

wheel to increase the electrical current sent to trolleys. Woods is sometimes credited as the inventor of the rail propulsion system called the third rail, though in truth, he followed several other thinkers who came up with similar concepts around the same time. The third rail is a method of supplying electricity to trains without using overhead power lines. Instead, workers built a new rail, which carried a powerful electric current and ran parallel to the existing track. Trains are then connected to the rail, giving them all the energy they need. The third rail is still a feature of many commuter train lines to this day.

Despite his undeniably brilliant inventions, Woods frequently had money problems. In 1885, five years after starting his company, he wrote, "I have been depending entirely upon daily labor and what money I could borrow."[30] Woods eventually sold several of his patents to large corporations. One of his earliest patents, which was for a telephone transmitter, was acquired by the Bell Telephone Company. The payments he received seem to have been relatively small, though, and Woods had difficulty making money on the patents he kept. He was never wealthy, nor did he even reach the financial status of the middle class.

Woods was also forced to defend himself against lawsuits brought by rivals who claimed he had stolen their ideas. Although Woods typically had fewer resources than the men who were suing him, he was largely able to defeat their challenges. Twice, Thomas Edison took Woods to court, claiming that Woods had infringed on one of his patents. Both times, Woods won the case. After the second time, recognizing Woods's skills and inventiveness, Edison offered Woods a job in his engineering department—a job Woods turned down, preferring to stay in business for himself. Even when Woods won a case, however, he could not celebrate his victory. Defending himself against the suits still cost him both money and time.

The Legacy of Skilled Inventors

Granville T. Woods died in 1910 at age 53. Though he had failed to make much money, he had made significant and lasting contributions to technology. Just as Latimer's work with electric lights helped make the Age of Electricity a reality, so too did Woods's improvements to telegraphs, telephones, and trains. Both inventors received plenty of

recognition from other African Americans, and each drew the attention of whites as well, in spite of widespread racial prejudice. One white journalist referred to Woods as "the greatest electrician in the world,"[31] and another wrote that Woods was "equal, if not superior, to any inventor in the country,"[32] regardless of race. The *New York Times* printed a brief obituary when Lewis Latimer died in 1928, an honor the paper's editors did not extend to previous African American inventors. Moreover, some white business leaders showed great respect for Latimer, both as an inventor and as a person, when they asked for his help in resolving patent disputes.

Despite their success and respect as scientists and inventors, neither Woods nor Latimer could diminish the racial prejudice in the United States. Even as many Americans saw two black men create incredible improvements to their daily lives, they believed that the African American population in general was inferior. Historian Rayvon Fouché argued that Latimer achieved success only because he downplayed his race. "Several times he was asked to speak out on racial issues and each time he said no. He was a conservative black man. It would have been hard for him to maintain his economic status and also be outspoken."[33] Many observers also believed that Woods had a number of "white" characteristics, which set him apart from most African Americans of his time in the largely prejudiced eyes of white Americans. "[Woods] is fluent in conversation," one white magazine reporter wrote, "and his speech is entirely free from [accent]."[34] Whites found it easier to categorize Woods and Latimer as outliers—examples of unusually skilled black men.

The accomplishments of Woods, Latimer, and other African Americans were both important and impressive. Many overcame prejudice, a lack of significant education, and poverty. They persisted in the face of hardship, and added enormously to the world's understanding of electricity and its uses. Though Americans in general gave them more attention and respect than earlier African American inventors had received, Latimer and Woods did not earn much money from their inventions, and their work brought them less fame than they deserved. The United States was not yet ready to make black inventors either truly rich or truly famous.

CHAPTER FOUR
PROGRESS IN THE 20TH CENTURY

Though the United States had been steadily moving toward increased acceptance of all races, it was doing so very slowly. While there is no question that the years after the Civil War saw a huge improvement to the lives of African Americans, there were still centuries of racial inequality and prejudice that needed to be overcome. At the turn of the 20th century, black people were still far behind other races in America in terms of wealth, education, and political power. However, thanks to the efforts of brilliant inventors, from Norbert Rillieux to Lewis Latimer, some Americans were beginning to see beyond race. In the early 1900s, black inventors were some of the most profitable and successful in history—and as their quality of life improved, they helped the entire African American community. They acquired both respect and wealth.

The foundations for this success were centuries in the making. The incredible inventions from other black inventors proved that they were just as thoughtful, intelligent, and resourceful as their white counterparts. Though Granville T. Woods died in poverty, one journalist wrote that he proved "beyond doubt the possibility of a colored man inventing as well as one of any other race."[35] However, the entire African American community as a whole is also largely responsible for the increasing prosperity of 20th century innovators. As black people saw the success of men, such as Jan Matzeliger and Lewis Latimer, who came from poverty and still demonstrated amazing abilities, they broke through some self-imposed racial barriers. Rather than buying into the idea that they belonged to a lower class, African Americans during this time came together to support one of their own in his or her success.

Black inventors of the early 20th century responded by uplifting the entire population.

A Hard Life Begins

Of all the great inventors of the early 1900s, the one with the most compelling story could be Sarah Breedlove, known to millions of her contemporaries as Madam C.J. Walker. Her life is particularly intriguing for several reasons. For one, Walker was not only an African American, she was also a woman. Given the sexist attitudes of the day, which existed among all races, Walker faced prejudice from two sides. Moreover, she had an extremely difficult early life, as many African Americans did, and most were unable to achieve monetary or social success after such a rocky start. Madam Walker was different, however, and her enormous prosperity is a testament to her intelligence and perseverance.

Sarah Breedlove was born in 1867 to poor former slaves who lived in Louisiana. Her early years were challenging. She was orphaned before she was 7, she married at 14 to escape an abusive brother-in-law, and by her early 20s, she was a widow with a young child to support. Trying to make a living and support her young child, she found work washing other people's clothes and sheets. This was a long and strenuous task in the days before automatic washers and dryers. For the next 15 years, the only major change in her life was a move from the rural South to St. Louis, Missouri, a city with greater economic opportunities, in addition to a thriving black culture. However, racism and sexism were still prevalent in St. Louis, and by 1890, it was difficult to imagine that she would ever have a better life.

Then, Walker's problems grew worse. In the 1890s, her hair began to fall out, leaving bald spots across her scalp. Hair loss was annoying and embarrassing, but it was not unusual for African American women of the time. Poor nutrition and stress were major contributors to the problem. The most important factor, however, was the way African American women treated their hair. The ideal of American beauty at the time called for women to have long, straight hair. This look was easy enough for many white women, but most black women had hair that was naturally short and curly. The only way for African American women to make their hair long and straight was to pull, twist, or stretch their hair. Over time, the twists and pulls stressed the scalp. Hair loss was one common result of this treatment.

With such a widespread problem, chemists and marketers had developed lotions, powders, and oils designed to prevent the loss of hair. These remedies were easy to find in African American sections of St. Louis and other cities. When Walker tried these concoctions, however, she was not impressed. Some of these oils and lotions contained ingredients that caused unpleasant side effects. Others stressed the hair and scalp even further, causing more damage. Few seemed to have any value at all.

The Growth of an Industry

Since these formulas had not stopped her hair loss, Walker resolved to come up with her own medication. She combined a variety of ingredients in dozens of different ways, hoping that each formula would fix her scalp problems. However, her mixes proved ineffective again and again. Around 1900, however, Walker had a breakthrough. As she told the story, she had a revelatory dream after a particularly frustrating day of experiments: "A big black man appeared to me and told me what to mix up for my hair. Some of the remedy was grown in Africa, but I sent for it, mixed it, put it on my scalp, and in a few weeks, my hair

was coming in faster than it had ever fallen out."[36]

Whether it was the result of a dream or the product of countless hours of experimentation, the new concoction did wonders for Walker's hair. Delighted, Walker shared her invention with her friends. The results were promising, and Walker soon developed other hair care products as well. In 1905, she moved to Denver, Colorado, and began going door-to-door, marketing her inventions directly to black women. At each house, she demonstrated her shampoos and oils on potential customers. Walker was confident that her product would help the majority of these women. She believed that after women saw what her products could do, they would be willing and eager to pay for more. Within a year of moving to Denver, she had married a newspaper worker named Charles J. Walker. When her business really took off, she marketed herself as Madam C.J. Walker.

Her new name and aggressive selling methods were successful. Word of her products spread quickly through Denver and beyond. With help from friends and family members, Walker opened a mail-order business. Then, she began making sales tours of the rural South, acquiring new customers through product demonstrations, just as she had in Denver. She advertised extensively as well, boasting about the effectiveness and efficiency of her goods. One advertisement promised, "Your hair will respond immediately. In one treatment it will be straight and fluffy."[37] Walker also established a network of African American women who sold her products and split the proceeds with her, helping many of them move toward the middle class. Her saleswomen had a serious interest in making the company prosper: As Walker made money, they made money.

By 1908, the name Madam C.J. Walker was familiar to black people all across the United States—and to many whites as well. As more and more customers tried Walker's remedies, sales soared. Before long, Walker was a millionaire. In fact, she was the first African American woman to achieve that status on her own. She once said in a speech, "I am a woman who came from the cotton fields of the South. From there I was promoted to the washtub ... And from there I promoted myself into the business of manufacturing hair goods and preparations ... I have built my own

Madam C.J. Walker's revolutionary hair care products made her wealthy and influential. She gave back to her community and assisted other African Americans.

MORE THAN AN INVENTOR

When Madam Walker died in 1919, her successors hired an African American beautician named Marjorie Joyner to run Walker's cosmetology schools. Joyner was a worthy successor to Walker as an inventor. In 1926, she designed an invention that she called a permanent waving machine. This machine consisted of a set of 16 metal rods, which were suspended from a circular hanger. The rods were placed in the hair and then heated. The heat curled hair that was already straight and straightened hair that was naturally curled. Joyner was issued a patent on her invention in 1928.

In addition to being an inventor and a business administrator, Joyner was also deeply involved in community and political issues. In 1935, for example, she became one of the founding members of an advocacy organization called the National Council of Negro Women. Throughout her career, she was a strong voice on behalf of black people in her home city of Chicago, Illinois. Her work brought her into close contact with a number of famous people, from educator Mary McLeod Bethune to former First Lady and activist Eleanor Roosevelt. As one reporter put it, Joyner went "practically everywhere and met practically everyone."[1] She died in 1994 at the age of 98, active in her community until the end of her life. She is remembered equally as an exceptional business-woman, thoughtful inventor, and passionate social activist.

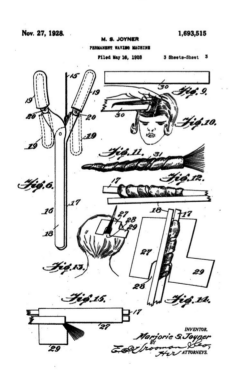

Marjorie Joyner's permanent waving machine, shown here, was a significant invention in the beauty industry and helped that industry evolve.

1. Adam Linder, "You Know, I'm 95 and I Know What I'm Talking About," *Chicago Reader*, September 10, 1992. www.chicagoreader.com/chicago/you-know-im-95-and-i-know-what-im-talking-about/Content?oid=880420.

factory on my own ground."[38]

After achieving such great wealth, Walker devoted much of her fortune to helping the people that had made her rich. Until the end of her life in 1919, she worked hard to educate young African Americans and help them achieve economic self-sufficiency. As a reporter for an Indiana newspaper wrote in 1918, "It is safe to say there is no one belonging to the colored race that is doing more for the education of boys and girls or is helping more struggling young men and women than Madam Walker."[39] Walker's creativity and inventiveness had lifted her out of poverty. By hiring thousands of black salespeople and employees, she helped do the same for countless other African Americans of her time.

Sewing Machines and Safety Masks

Though Madam C.J. Walker's rise from poverty to success was incredible, it was paralleled by another contemporary black inventor—a man named Garrett Morgan. In some ways, Morgan's story is similar to Walker's. Born in Kentucky in 1877, Morgan, like Walker, was the child of freed slaves. Like Walker, too, Morgan had little formal education and was forced to leave home at an early age to try to make his way in the world. While Walker made a name for herself through hair care products, Morgan's interests were in machinery. At just 14, he found work as a handyman in Cincinnati, Ohio. A few years later he relocated to Cleveland, where he got a job repairing sewing machines.

Morgan's job provided him with stability and a steady paycheck. It gave him no opportunity to advance, however, and Morgan—again like Madam Walker—had ambitions for his life. In 1907, after intensely studying the internal mechanisms of sewing machines, he left his job and opened his own business repairing and selling them. He was issued a patent for an improved machine, which would work quicker and break less often. Soon, he married a Bavarian immigrant named Mary Anne Hassek, and her experience as a seamstress allowed their business to expand into tailoring as well. By 1912, he had several dozen employees. With his business experiencing success, he devoted more and more of his time to tinkering with machinery and devising and building new inventions. An extremely creative man, he impressed others with the wide range of his unique and useful ideas. "He had all these things in his head that just had to come out,"[40] his granddaughter recalled.

Morgan also invented a gas mask, which he called a safety hood. He built the earliest working model of the mask in 1912 and was issued a patent for it two years later. Intended for firefighters and other emergency personnel, the safety hood filtered dangerous particles (such as soot and dust) from the air, enabling the wearer to inhale fresh oxygen even while surrounded by smoke. Morgan wrote in his patent application that a rescue worker who wore the device could "enter a house filled with thick suffocating gases" and still "breathe freely for some time."[41] Morgan noted that the mask could also be useful for chemists and others who worked in situations where the air might be unsafe to breathe normally.

An Invention to Save Lives

It did not take long for the public to hear about this revolutionary mask. In July 1916, a pocket of natural gas exploded in a work tunnel beneath Lake Erie, near Morgan's home in Cleveland. "The tunnel was turned into a death hole in a twinkling [very quickly],"[42] a newspaper reported in nearby Sandusky, Ohio. Workers close to the tunnel entrance quickly climbed to the surface, but toxic gases and billowing smoke sealed off the escape route for workers on the far side of the explosion. Several men went into the tunnel, hoping to reach the victims and carry them out. However, the fumes and gases were more toxic than they knew. Once underground, the suffocating smoke also overcame most of the rescuers. Only a few managed to return safely to the surface. The rest were trapped or killed.

The situation looked bleak. "Not a vestige of hope remains that any of the prisoners will be brought to the surface alive,"[43] a local reporter wrote. However, someone at the scene of the accident knew that Garrett Morgan lived nearby. He was quickly brought to the site, where he and his brother put on their masks and took up the task of searching for survivors. Breathing filtered air through their masks, the two men made their way into the tunnel.

Once they were underground, they found some men were already dead. They did eventually find one worker who was still alive. As Morgan recalled, the rescuers "discovered from [his] groans"[44] that this worker had not yet been killed by the smoke and gas. The brothers hurriedly carried him to safety and returned to see if there were others. It is unclear exactly how many men Garrett and his brother were able to save, but it is

Garrett Morgan's heroic rescue efforts demonstrated not just his personal bravery, but also his personal genius. He invented a device that could save thousands of lives all over the world.

He was about to be recognized at a national level and experience some of the prosperity that came with that recognition.

Success in the Face of Unmasked Racism

Following the episode under Lake Erie, fire departments and rescue workers across the United States wanted to buy masks of their own. Morgan was happy to fulfill as many orders as he could. Unfortunately, just like the racial prejudice that Elijah McCoy faced years earlier, the leaders of some of these organizations canceled their orders when they discovered that the inventor was black. According to a biography of Morgan, "Apparently, many people would rather face danger and possibly death than rely on a lifesaving device created by a

evident that it was at least two. They did recover the bodies of all the dead. Despite the nature of the tragic events, Garrett Morgan's safety hood was demonstrated in a very public way.

A Fresh State

Though Iowa State had accepted Carver as a student, most American colleges at the time were not so progressive. Many were like the Kansas college that Carver had tried to attend: No black applicants were admitted. As a result, African American leaders had established schools of higher learning specifically intended for African Americans. These schools provided young black people with a place to continue their education after high school. However, they were seriously under-funded. Many were too poor to pay for basic sup-plies. Because they could not pay their teachers well or keep their buildings in good repair, all-black col-leges were simply not at the same level as colleges that were mainly white.

One of the best known of these historically African American schools was Tuskegee Normal and Industrial Institute in Tuskegee, Alabama. A black leader named Booker T. Washington had founded this school, known most often sim-ply as Tuskegee Institute,

in 1881. In 1896, Washington saw Carver as an opportunity to upgrade his school's faculty. He invited Carver to operate Tuskegee's new agriculture department. "I cannot offer you money, position, or fame," Washington wrote in a letter to Carver. "These things I now ask you to give up." However, even if the job did not reward him with money, Washington thought, Carver might still consider it out of a sense of

Famed African American leader Booker T. Washington persuaded the young and brilliant George Washington Carver to work at his Tuskegee Institute. It is there that Carver did most of his life's work.

responsibility to his fellow African Americans. "I offer you," Washington wrote, "the task of bringing a people from degradation, poverty, and waste to full manhood."[50]

Washington's request was persuasive. Carver accepted the appointment, and he spent the rest of his career at Tuskegee. As a departmental leader, he used his knowledge of soils, crops, and agricultural techniques to assist poor farmers, particularly African Americans, in the South. His first success was reducing farmers' dependence on cotton. Though cotton was an important cash crop in the South at the time, it had been taking the nutrients out of the soil, since it was planted in the same fields for years. Each season, the land produced less cotton, cutting farmers' already low incomes. Carver taught farmers how to restore nutrients to the earth by planting crops such as peanuts, peas, and sweet potatoes in rotation with cotton.

Fixing Farming

Carver's new crop rotations were a major help to rural southern farmers. Not only was their cotton production increased, they had more edible crops to harvest. These methods created an oversupply of sweet potatoes, peanuts, and peas. At the time, these foods made up only a small part of most southerners' diets. Rather than let these crops go to waste in the fields, Carver spent countless hours in his laboratory devising new uses for them. His creativity and his thorough understanding of biology and chemistry helped him create and design many products made from these crops. He is best remembered today for his work with peanuts. He was able to turn them into such unlikely goods as cheese, ink, linoleum, and soap. He also successfully synthesized vinegar, flour, and much more from sweet potatoes.

When Carver died in 1943, he left behind an incredible number of new farming techniques, new scientific understanding, and—most of all—new products. His research and experimentation resulted in more than 300 new uses for the peanut and more than 100 for the sweet potato. Carver's creative innovations extended to other materials as well. At the beginning of World War II, for example, he developed roughly 500 shades of dye. This was helpful to the United States because the war had cut Americans off from their usual sources of dyes in Europe. He crossbred plants to create resilient crops that would produce more food. He found new uses for cornstalks, created a variety of products from soybeans and cotton, and became "the

HUNDREDS OF USES FOR PEANUTS

Today, George Washington Carver is best remembered as a man whose scientific and creative mind had no limits. From the simple peanut and sweet potato, crops that few people thought had any value, he was able to derive hundreds of products. Among these products were: pancake flour, meat substitutes, chili sauce, dry coffee, cream candy, mayonnaise, Worcestershire sauce, cooking oil, salad oil, vinegar, buttermilk, cream cheese, cocoa, pickles, butterscotch, caramel, laundry soap, rubbing oil, hand lotion, shampoo, vanishing cream, shaving cream, antiseptic soap, colored paper, glue, gasoline, plastic, metal polish, shoe blacking, and linoleum. Even this huge list is just a small fraction of what Carver's genius produced.

first scientist to make synthetic marble from wood shavings."[51]

Booker T. Washington's prediction that Carver would sacrifice money by moving to Tuskegee did turn out to be accurate. During Carver's lifetime, U.S. law did not permit inventors to patent most items created from plants. Since nearly all of Carver's work was derived from agriculture, he had no way of obtaining exclusive rights to his creations. It seems clear, too, that other institutions might have been able to pay him a higher salary than he was able to earn at Tuskegee. However, money never seemed important to Carver. According to some sources, Carver rarely accepted raises when Tuskegee offered them. He was interested in innovation for its own sake. He never achieved wealth from his work.

However, Washington was wrong when he said that Carver would have to sacrifice his chance at fame if he came to Tuskegee. On the contrary, Carver became one of the most famous and respected scientists of his time. Carmaker Henry Ford befriended him, and so did fellow inventor Thomas Edison. Carver spoke on farm policy to the U.S. Congress, was frequently interviewed by newspaper and magazine reporters, and won many important awards and honors. When he died, he was mourned all across the United States. His death was a blow to both blacks and whites. "Nature chose well when she picked this great Negro to carry on her work,"[52] a Nevada newspaper proclaimed on the day following Carver's death. Even though he was a black man in an age of widespread discrimination, his outstanding work earned him respect from people of all races.

A Nation Changing

In the early 20th century, African Americans had difficulty achieving fame or fortune in any field. Though they had been enjoying greater freedoms for nearly 50 years, they rarely, if ever, had the same opportunities that most Americans had. In education, in politics, and in business, black people were given little chance to succeed. Like other African Americans who acted on their ambitions, Madam C.J. Walker, Garrett Morgan, and George Washington Carver all experienced poverty and racial discrimination. However, despite the challenges, all three achieved long-lasting success. Much of this success was due to their own qualities as individual humans and as talented inventors. Few Americans, from any time or of any race, could match these three for ingenuity, intelligence, and drive.

The remarkable success stories of Walker, Morgan, and Carver had another cause, as well. Even in the face of prejudice and hostility from other Americans, black people were beginning to establish systems and institutions of their own. By 1900, large numbers of African Americans remained very poor. However, when members of the black community saw someone succeeding, they banded together and had enough buying power to make them a millionaire, as was the case with Madam C.J. Walker. By 1900, lack of education was still a serious concern in the black community. However, some educated African Americans were increasingly able to set up scientific labs, publish newspapers aimed at black readers, and raise the level of education at new black colleges and universities. Black America in the early 1900s was ready to create its own heroes and heroines. It did so by recognizing and helping some of its brightest minds: the African American inventors of the era.

CHAPTER FIVE
CHANGING ATTITUDES, CHANGING TECHNOLOGY

From the rise of slavery to the end of the Civil War to the turn of the 20th century, the progress of African Americans in society has been increasing for more than 100 years. From the 1950s to today, more black people have risen to the middle class, have earned college degrees, and have become a crucial part of society in the United States. The country even had a black president for two consecutive terms; the days when black people were not even allowed to vote seem to be in the distant past. Despite these improvements, things are far from being perfectly equal. There has undoubtedly been improvement in the lives of many African Americans, but they are still rarely offered the same level of opportunity as white Americans. One researcher concluded, "not all children are benefiting equally from the American dream."[53] African American inventors have been trying to change this for many years.

Black scientists and inventors were able to enjoy increased acceptance by Americans in general beginning near the middle of the 20th century. After hundreds of inventions, such as Garrett Morgan's safety hood, that improved the lives of every race, many Americans were beginning to understand that black people had just as much potential as any person. People were no longer basing their purchasing decisions on the race of the product's inventor. Racial prejudice was finally beginning to die down—and African Americans took advantage of this new opportunity. Another new wave of innovation and ingenuity arrived. Black inventors rose to the occasion, and in the time period beginning in the 1950s and still going on today, their work has improved the lives of people worldwide.

Orphan and Mechanic

One of the first of these modern African American inventors was a man named Frederick McKinley Jones. He was a remarkable inventor whose talents were equal to those of Elijah McCoy or Thomas Edison. During his long career as an innovator, Jones developed a variety of new devices, from an automatic ticket-taking mechanism to a new type of portable X-ray machine. The majority of Jones's inventions, however, had to do with refrigeration and cooling. Indeed, Jones's work in this field remains an important part of modern society's use of cooling devices.

Jones's life, like the lives of many contemporary African Americans, was not easy. Born in Cincinnati on May 17, 1893, Jones had a tragic childhood. His mother died when he was very young. His father had trouble raising the young boy and sent him to live with a Catholic priest when he was 7 or 8 years old. As a teenager, Jones left the church and tried to support himself. Though he had not received even a high school education, he was deeply interested in mechanics. He soon got a job as a janitor in a Cincinnati car repair shop. Before long, his talents took him to the position of foreman. Even though he had some success in Cincinnati, Jones moved to Hallock, Minnesota, where he took a job as chief mechanic for a wealthy farmer.

Over the next few years, Jones read as much as he could about engineering and electronics, hoping to develop his mechanical knowledge. He also became an enthusiastic automobile racer. After he briefly joined the military during World War I, Jones returned to Minnesota, where he built a transmitter for Hallock's radio station, designed a portable X-ray machine for Hallock's doctors, and developed new technologies for the soundtracks of movies. By the late 1920s, Jones had become the local expert on mechanics and engineering.

Films and Refrigeration

At this point in his life, Jones was unknown outside of Hallock. His incredible talents were soon discovered, however, because of his work with movies. In the early 20th century, movies had no recorded sound due to technical limitations. Because of this, characters rarely spoke. When they did need to have some dialogue, the film would show a card with the written words on it. These were called intertitles, or title cards. In the 1920s, however, it became possible to synchronize recorded sound with the action on the screen; the first films with sound were called "talkies." These movies became very popular among audiences. Theater owners now had to either quickly acquire technology that could play these new films or go out of business as their competitors did.

After the emergence of movies with sound, a theater owner in Hallock hired Jones to design a system that could play movie soundtracks. Though Jones had no experience with this kind of work and little money to work with, he accepted the job. Before long, he designed and built a device that not only played sound, but improved the quality of the projected film as well. Word of Jones's outstanding talents soon spread to Minneapolis, the largest city in the state, and to a businessman named Joe Numero. As the owner of a company that produced machines for the theater and movie industry, Numero thought Jones would be an outstanding addition to his staff. In the late 1920s, he hired Jones and brought him to Minneapolis.

Over the next few years, Jones did more than his fair share of work for Numero's company. He came up with improvements to the company's existing technologies and developed a few new technologies of his own. In the 1930s, his career took an unexpected turn when Numero got into a discussion with a fellow businessman who was in the trucking business. This man, named Harry Werner, was complaining about the difficulty of keeping food cold while it was being transported. This was a common problem at the time, as mobile refrigeration technology was still undeveloped. Numero claimed that his employee, Jones, with his impressive mechanical abilities, could build something that would solve the problem.

Despite this boast, it is likely that Numero was joking with Werner. Fortunately, Jones was actually enthusiastic about fixing this problem. "We ought to be able to fix up something,"[54] he told Numero after examining a shipping truck. Despite Jones's limited education, his difficulty obtaining materials, and his lack of experience with heating and cooling engineering, he eventually came up with a refrigeration unit that could keep the inside of a truck cold enough to transport fresh goods. Jones showed his invention to Numero, who immediately saw the device's potential. Deciding to

*Modern in-truck refrigeration units, such as the one shown
here, are still based on Frederick Jones's original designs
and improvements.*

Control Company; they later renamed it Thermo King Corporation. Their goal was to develop, manufacture, and distribute Jones's refrigeration units for trucks.

Refrigeration Royalty

Despite the incredible technology, Thermo King was not an immediate success. Numero said in an interview, "we had to sweat like hell to start this business."[55] Still, after Jones was issued a patent for his refrigeration unit in 1940, the device slowly became the standard for trucking compa-

switch his focus from sound systems to refrigeration, Numero sold his film supply company and formed a business partnership with Jones. They founded a new corporation, originally named the U.S. Thermo

nies across the United States. The invention allowed truckers to ship perishable food safely, even during the hottest weather. This made it possible for food produced in Rhode Island or New York to be eaten in

Texas or California. One newspaper wrote, Jones's invention "eliminated the problem of spoilage [and] revolutionized the eating habits of Americans."[56]

Jones followed his device with similar innovations meant for refrigerating trains and ships, along with an air conditioning unit meant for hospitals, several improvements to truck refrigeration technology, and many other inventions. In all, he earned more than 60 patents before his death in 1961. Despite this, Jones never received much notice from the general public for his work. Though his inventions directly impacted their lives, his products were mainly sold for commercial, rather than consumer, purposes. Even so, other scientists and technicians respected his accomplishments. During World War II, for instance, Jones's cooling units were widely used to keep blood and medicine from spoiling as they were shipped to the front lines. The military was happy to acknowledge the system's inventor. "We are particularly grateful for the work of Mr. Fred Jones,"[57] an army official wrote in a letter to Numero. The Thermo King Corporation also saw huge profits during Jones's lifetime.

Even those who appreciated Jones's work, though, could not forget that he was black. Journalists who profiled him or mentioned him in their articles almost always highlighted his race. One 1951 news article about Jones's achievements referred to the "inventive genius of [this] soft-spoken Negro engineer."[58] By doing this, the media and the public thought of Jones in the same way they had thought of Morgan, Walker, and other inventors of the previous generation, leading with his race and putting his job as an engineer behind that. However, the use of phrases such as "inventive genius" highlight the fact that a shift toward a more modern way of thinking about race was happening. The way Jones was treated was evidence that the majority of Americans were increasingly willing to give credit where it was due, even if they were not ready to go completely beyond racial boundaries yet.

A Creative Chemist

Jones's work with refrigeration made him one of the most important African American inventors of the 20th century. His achievements were matched in a different field by Percy Julian, a scientist who was issued dozens of patents in the field of chemistry. Born in Alabama in

DOCTORS AND INNOVATORS

Charles Drew was an African American doctor who became well known during the 1930s and 1940s for his work in blood transfusion. Blood transfusion is when blood is taken from one person and given to a patient who is very sick or who has suffered physical trauma. While not technically an inventor, Drew is credited with several medical innovations. He was the first to set up so-called blood banks, where blood plasma (the liquid part of the blood) could be stored until needed. These blood banks proved particularly useful during World War II. By keeping the plasma fresh, military doctors could save the lives of soldiers injured in battle, even when there was no time to evacuate them to a regular hospital.

Charles Drew was an early researcher and experimenter in human blood transfusions. His work laid the foundations for many lifesaving procedures.

Drew was not the first innovative African American doctor. In 1893, Daniel Hale Williams became the first physician to successfully perform open-heart surgery, which is an operation on the heart itself. The world believed this kind of surgery was impossible before Williams managed to carry it out. It has since become standard practice for surgeons. Like Drew, Williams may not have been an inventor as the word is understood today. Nevertheless, both of these men were pioneers who were tremendously helpful to Americans of all races, both then and now.

1899, Julian was an intelligent child whose parents were determined to get him an education. Though few African American children of that era went to school beyond sixth grade, Julian completed high school and then enrolled in DePauw University, a school in Indiana, to study science.

Julian's years at DePauw were a struggle. The college refused to house him in a dormitory, and because he was black, it was difficult for him to find a place to stay in the surrounding town. A friend eventually helped him find work in a fraternity house, where he "fired the furnace for room and waited tables for board."[59] Academics were a struggle for Julian at first, too. His all-black high school did not cover all the material DePauw expected incoming students to know. Consequently, Julian began at a much lower level than his classmates and was required to take remedial classes for no credit before he could learn at the same level as regular students. Once Julian made up his missing coursework, however, he excelled. When he graduated from DePauw in 1920, he was first in his class.

Upon earning his bachelor's degree, Julian was eager to continue to graduate school. He hoped to earn a doctorate in chemistry, despite the fact that only one other African American had ever been awarded one. His academic record certainly suggested that he could be the second to do so. Some of his professors, however, tried to talk him out of pursuing this goal. Few graduate schools would even consider admitting a black student; even if one did, they pointed out, Julian's job prospects would be bleak. Students who earned doctorates typically went on to teach at colleges and universities, but Julian's professors warned him that he would find employment only at all-black schools. Other colleges, they said, would never consider giving him a job as an instructor. In their eyes, white students would refuse to learn from an African American, no matter how intelligent or qualified he was. If he wanted to teach, and only African American universities would hire him, he did not need more than a bachelor's degree.

At first, Julian listened to their suggestions and warnings. He taught briefly at Fisk University, an all-black school in Tennessee. Though it was a prestigious school for black students, it was underfunded and overcrowded. After two years, he discovered that Harvard University, one of the greatest schools in

DEPAUW UNIVERSITY: FROM INTOLERANCE TO ACCEPTANCE

James Julian, Percy Julian's father, had always wanted to attend a university. He believed that continuing education was the way for any person to get ahead in society—even a black person. Unfortunately for him, he was born a generation too soon to achieve his dream; the racial prejudice his son experienced was just a fraction of what James went through. As a young boy in Alabama, James Julian attended a school run by a religious organization. One of his teachers was from Indiana and was familiar with DePauw University. Noting James's intelligence and desire for knowledge, she once remarked with obvious regret that he would most likely never be able to attend a college. It was only his race that kept him away.

Though James never did attend college, his teacher's support stayed with him throughout his life. Her words helped him guide Percy toward higher education and DePauw. Though Percy's DePauw experience was not entirely positive, James and his wife then sent their next four children—Mattie, Elizabeth, Irma, and Emerson—to the school as well. All four received their degrees between 1926 and 1938.

The only Julian child who did not graduate from DePauw was James Jr., the youngest in the family. He initially enrolled at DePauw, but he soon transferred to the University of Chicago, where he earned his bachelor's degree. He later earned a medical degree from Howard University. In 1970, however, when James Jr. was 68 years old, DePauw officials awarded him an honorary bachelor's degree. This year was significant because it marked both "the 100th anniversary of the birth of [James Jr.'s] father and the 50th anniversary of Percy Julian's ... graduation in 1920."[1]

1. "DePauw Will Graduate 6th in Family," *Anderson Herald* (Anderson, IN), May 22, 1970.

the world, would accept him as a graduate student. He earned his master's degree after one year, and by 1923, he was ready to continue his education. Julian's excitement was cut short, though, when Harvard officials denied his application to enter their doctoral program. Most Ph.D. programs required candidates to teach low-level courses or assist professors, and Harvard decided that no African American could teach their primarily white students. Though Julian did earn a master's degree at Harvard, his dream was to earn his doctorate. He left the university in the face of racial prejudice to continue his education elsewhere.

In 1929, Julian left the United States for Vienna, Austria, where prejudice against blacks was less significant and where the local university was happy to have him as a student. In Vienna, Julian did important research into medical chemistry, some of it alongside a European student named Josef Pikl. Two years later, after finally receiving his doctoral degree, Percy Julian returned to the United States. In the early 1930s, he accepted a position as a chemistry professor at DePauw—the same school where professors had only recently told him that white students would never accept a black instructor. Attitudes were beginning to change.

Groundbreaking Chemical Research

While teaching at DePauw, Julian continued his research and chemical experimentation. Much of his initial work concentrated on a chemical compound called physostigmine. This substance appears naturally in a plant known as the Calabar bean. Scientists knew that if someone could find a way to extract physostigmine, several diseases could be treated more easily. These included glaucoma, an eye disease that can lead to blindness, and an immune system disorder named myasthenia gravis. However, it was difficult and expensive to naturally extract physostigmine from the Calabar bean. Julian tried to develop ways to synthesize the chemical. Synthesizing a compound means manufacturing it in a laboratory, and synthesized compounds are typically cheaper to produce. He worked on this problem with Pikl, who had come with him from Vienna and joined him at DePauw to solve this chemical problem. In 1935, Julian and Pikl successfully created an artificial form of physostigmine. Their incredible chemical discovery is still used in the treatment of glaucoma and other diseases today.

Shortly after making a name for himself with the synthesis of physostigmine, Julian moved to Chicago to work in private industry. He used proteins derived from soybeans

Percy Julian is one of the most accomplished chemists in American history.

to produce artificial human hormones from soybean plants and other materials. Like the physostigmine Julian developed in the lab at DePauw, these hormones had important medical uses. Cortisone, one of these hormones, was used in the treatment of rheumatoid arthritis. Others helped cancer patients or reduced the chances of miscarriage in pregnancy. Julian was able to obtain patents for many of the processes he developed to create these drugs.

By any standard, and especially compared to black inventors from earlier time periods, Percy Julian was enormously successful. In 1953, he founded his own business, which he sold eight years later to a large pharmaceutical company for more than $2 million. When he died in 1975, he

to improve and create a variety of products. These ranged from such basic materials as glue and paint to a new kind of foam used to extinguish fires during World War II. Before long, Julian had figured out a way

RACIAL POLITICS

George Washington Murray was an African American from Sumter County, South Carolina. Born in 1853, he began his life as a slave. He eventually became a farmer, teacher, and inventor, holding eight patents on various types of farm tools. He is better known today, however, for his political career. Despite laws and customs that limited the right of African Americans to vote, Murray was elected twice to the United States House of Representatives. He served from 1893 to 1897, and he was the only black member of Congress at this time.

Murray had a deep appreciation for black history and a desire to improve the lives of African Americans of his own time. He worked to highlight the achievements of African Americans, both past and present. In one notable instance,

he made a speech in Congress, asking for the work of African Americans to be included in a proposed celebration of southern technology and scientific progress. "The colored people of this country," he said, "want an opportunity to show that ... they, too, are part and parcel of [our] great civilization."[1] He ended his speech by reading aloud a list of 92 black inventors and their achievements, a list that has provided a starting point for many students of black history.

1. Quoted in David L. Fordham, *True Stories of Black South Carolina*. Charleston, SC: The History Press, 2008.

Despite being born a slave, George Washington Murray was able to pull himself up and become a highly successful inventor and politician.

held more than 100 patents, including some that had directly improved the health of thousands of sick people. Julian was well respected by his fellow scientists, and by others as well. Readers of a Chicago newspaper voted him Chicago's man of the year in 1950. In 1973, he became one of the first African Americans to be elected to the National Academy of Sciences. His synthesis of physostigmine was named one of America's top 25 chemical accomplishments of all time.

In spite of his brilliant talent, Julian's road to success was not entirely smooth. Racial prejudice was an issue throughout his life. Even in the 1950s, after his enormous success, when Julian moved his family to the wealthy, white Chicago suburb of Oak Park, an unknown criminal set his house on fire and threw dynamite onto his property in an effort to force him out of the community. Nonetheless, Julian's career, especially in the 1960s and 1970s, allowed many Americans to look past his skin color. Because of the more progressive time period he lived in, he was able to improve outside opinions of African Americans more than perhaps any other black inventor. A reporter in Chicago once wrote, "I've heard people remark that Dr. Julian is a credit to his race. I'd like to correct that statement. He's a credit to the HUMAN race!"[60] Similarly, one newspaper article about Julian that appeared shortly after his death did not mention Julian's race until the seventh paragraph. In the opening of the piece, the reporter characterized him simply as "an internationally known research chemist."[61] Slowly but surely, African Americans were receiving more equal recognition for their accomplishments.

A Future of Innovation

Many more generations of African American inventors have followed in the footsteps of Frederick McKinley Jones and Percy Julian. Otis Boykin, born in 1920, was among the first of these new inventors. Just one generation younger than Julian, Boykin held a variety of patents, and most of his work was with electrical equipment. Some of his patents were for electronic resistors, which prevent too much electricity from flowing into an appliance. He also created a new type of air filter and patented a cash register that he claimed was burglarproof. Boykin is best known today for an invention he built that helped heart patients. Some people have a heart condition that gives them an irregular heartbeat. Small devices, called pacemakers, help even out their heartbeats by using small electrical signals. While Boykin did not invent the pacemaker, he did develop a control unit that helped to make the pacemaker more usable and less dangerous.

Meredith Gourdine was another outstanding inventor, and he was also a remarkable athlete. Born in 1929, Gourdine won a silver medal in the long jump at the 1952 Olympics. After earning a Ph.D. in engineering science in 1960, he went on to patent more than 30 new devices. His inventions included a method of cooling computer chips, a way to convert coal into electricity, and a system for clearing smoke and fog from the air. Gourdine is also an interesting historical figure because, unlike almost every black inventor who preceded him, he had little difficulty getting a high quality education. Gourdine was offered a scholarship by the University of Michigan, graduated from Cornell University, and earned his Ph.D. at the California Institute of Technology. When he was attending college in the 1950s, prejudice against African Americans in education was not gone by any means, but Gourdine's story illustrates that the barriers were falling more and more rapidly.

In modern times, African Americans have continued to invent. For a time, many of these inventors were connected to the U.S. space program in some way. The National Aeronautics and Space Administration (NASA) employed a black man named Robert Shurney in the 1970s. He devised lightweight tires for NASA's lunar rover vehicle and a waste management system for use on Skylab, America's first space station. George E. Alcorn, born in 1940, is known for his work with new scientific imaging machines, some of which were used by NASA in the search for other life in space. George Carruthers helped design a specialized camera that could take pictures on a lunar mission; he also built a device that could detect electromagnetic radiation. NASA scientist Valerie Thomas invented a method for using a series of mirrors to create a three-dimensional illusion of a distant object.

Despite these inventors' successes working with NASA, space is by no means the only area of expertise for modern black inventors. Mark Dean, born in 1957, is the owner of several important patents relating to home computers. Ophthalmologist (eye doctor) Patricia Bath pioneered a way to use advanced laser technology in eye surgery. Shirley Ann Jackson began her career as a theoretical physicist before contributing to the invention of solar power cells and caller ID. There have been thousands of successful African American inventors in the modern era, and their innovations have ranged from cutting-edge technology to fun novelties, such as the "T-shirt with removable sleeves convertible to a hat."[62] With more equal opportunities, a sharp decline in racism, and an invincible inventive spirit, there is no doubt that African Americans will continue innovating and changing the world for the better.

Frequently asked to speak at events, Shirley Ann Jackson is an inventor, scientist, and the president of the Rensselaer Polytechnic Institute, a prestigious American college.

At the same time, the fact that inventions by African Americans are now common has had a somewhat unfortunate side effect. While some historians and educators have worked to uncover and highlight the accomplishments of past African American inventors such as Lewis Latimer, Madam C.J. Walker, and Elijah McCoy, the black inventors of today are not talked about as much as those who came before them.

In the past, widespread racial prejudice in the United States created significant obstacles and dangers for nearly every black inventor. The story of early black invention is largely a story of people who overcame serious hardships—hardships caused mainly by an environment they could not control.

In contrast, the racism of today's America is much less widespread and intrusive, and therefore, much less of an obstacle. As a result, the stories of today's black inventors are almost totally identical to the stories of inventors of any other race. In today's society, what matters more than anything is whether there is a good idea and the talent to back it up. Skin color has become less important than it was even 50 years ago.

The United States is continuing to progress to the point where only inventors exist, without having to be labeled African American, white, or any other race. The innovative spirit has often emerged victorious against racial prejudice, in large part thanks to the outstanding work of black inventors of the past and present.

NOTES

Chapter One: Pre-Civil War Black Inventors

1. James Mitchell, *Answer of the Agent of the Indiana Colonization Society*. Indianapolis, IN: Chapman, 1852, p. 15.
2. Portia P. James, *The Real McCoy: African American Invention and Innovation, 1619–1930*. Washington, DC: Smithsonian, 1989, p. 54.
3. Quoted in James, *The Real McCoy*, p. 53.
4. Quoted in James, *The Real McCoy*, p. 53.
5. Quoted in Sidney Kaplan, *American Studies in Black and White: Selected Essays, 1949–1989*. Boston, MA: University of Massachusetts Press, 1996, p. 232.
6. Quoted in Kaplan, *American Studies in Black and White*, p. 229.
7. Quoted in "Peake, George," The Encyclopedia of Cleveland History. ech.cwru.edu/ech-cgi/article.pl?id=PG.
8. Quoted in James, *The Real McCoy*, p. 40.
9. "Reward of Perseverance," *Weekly Wisconsin* (Milwaukee, WI), October 13, 1847.
10. Quoted in "Important Ohio Tester Bed, Henry Boyd, Cincinnati," Cowan's Auctions. www.cowanauctions.com/lot/important-ohio-tester-bed-henry-boyd-cincinnati-36486.
11. Michael W. Markowitz and Delores D. Jones-Brown, *The System in Black and White: Exploring the Connections between Race, Crime, and Justice*. Santa Barbara, CA: Greenwood, 2000, p. 141.

Chapter Two: Mechanical Experimentation and the Industrial Revolution

12. Allan Nevins and Henry Steele Commager, *A Pocket History of the United States*. New York, NY: Pocket Books, 1976, p. 258.
13. Quoted in Mark Aldrich, *Death Rode the Rails: American Railroad Accidents and Safety, 1828–1965*. Baltimore, MD: Johns Hopkins University Press, 2006, p. 104.
14. Quoted in C.R. Gibbs, *Black Inventors: From Africa to America: Two Million Years of Invention and Innovation*. Silver Spring, MD: Three Dimensional Publications, 1995.
15. "Pullman Company Sued," *Janesville Gazette* (Janesville, WI), January 28, 1892.

16. Quoted in Bruce Sinclair, ed., *Technology and the African-American Experience: Needs and Opportunities for Study.* Cambridge, MA: MIT Press, 2004, p. 58.

17. Quoted in John Sibley Butler, *Entrepreneurship and Self-Help Among Black Americans: A Reconsideration of Race and Economics.* Albany, NY: State University of New York Press, 1991, p. 60.

18. "Negro Inventor Versatile," *La Crosse Tribune* (La Crosse, WI), May 30, 1926, p. 6.

19. Quoted in Elaine Nembhard, "Black Inventor Alters Shoe Industry in U.S.," *Ocala Star-Banner* (Ocala, FL), December 25, 1981.

20. Patricia Carter Sluby, *The Inventive Spirit of African Americans: Patented Ingenuity.* Santa Barbara, CA: Greenwood, 2004, p. 40.

21. Quoted in United States Industrial Commission, *Report of the Industrial Commission*, vol. 14, Washington, DC: Government Printing Office, 1901, p. 302.

22. James, *The Real McCoy*, p. 72.

Chapter Three: Electric America

23. Charles Panati, *Panati's Extraordinary Origins of Everyday Things.* New York, NY: Harper & Row, 1987, p. 136.

24. Charles R. Brooks, "Black Inventor Helped Develop Telephone, Electric Lighting," *The News* (Frederick, MD), February 10, 1971, p. 10.

25. Quoted in Sluby, *The Inventive Spirit of African Americans*, p. 46.

26. Quoted in Kareem Abdul-Jabbar and Alan Steinberg, *Black Profiles in Courage.* New York, NY: Perennial, 1996, p. 210.

27. Quoted in Francis Jehl, *Menlo Park Reminiscences: Part 2.* Dearborn, MI: Edison's Institute, 1939, p. 708.

28. Quoted in Brooks, "Black Inventor Helped Develop Telephone, Electric Lighting," p. 10.

29. Quoted in Rayvon Fouché, *Black Inventors in the Age of Segregation: Granville T. Woods, Lewis H. Latimer & Shelby J. Davidson.* Baltimore, MD: Johns Hopkins University Press, 2003, p. 35.

30. Quoted in Fouché, *Black Inventors in the Age of Segregation*, p. 33.

31. Quoted in James, *The Real McCoy*, p. 95.

32. Quoted in Butler, *Entrepreneurship and Self-Help Among Black Americans*, p. 60.

33. Quoted in Teresa Riordan, "Patents; By Correcting Inaccuracies, a Professor Tries to Deliver a Fuller Picture of the Lives of African-American Inventors," *New York Times*, January 19, 2004. www.nytimes.com/2004/01/19/business/patents-correcting-

inaccuracies-professor-tries-deliver-fuller-picture-lives.html?_r=0.

34. S.W. Balch, "Electric Motor Regulation," *Cosmopolitan*, April 1895, p. 761.

Chapter Four: Progress in the 20th Century

35. Quoted in Butler, *Entrepreneurship and Self-Help Among Black Americans*, p. 60.

36. Quoted in Ayana D. Byrd and Lori L. Tharps, *Hair Story: Untangling the Roots of Black Hair in America*. New York, NY: St. Martin's, 2001, p. 34.

37. Quoted in "Death of Negress Revives Romance," *Waterloo Evening Courier* (Waterloo, IA), July 14, 1919.

38. Quoted in Madam C.J. Walker: The Official Web Site. www.madamcjwalker.com/#&panel1-1.

39. "Madam Walker at Mt. Olive Baptist Church," *Fort Wayne Journal-Gazette* (Fort Wayne, IN), March 12, 1918.

40. Quoted in Susan B. Griffith, "Children Raise Funds for Morgan Marker," *Cleveland Call & Post*, July 21, 1994.

41. Quoted in Gaius Chamberlain, "Garrett Morgan," The Black Inventor Online Museum, March 23, 2012. blackinventor.com/garrett-morgan/.

42. "Twenty-three Dead in Tunnel Under Lake?" *Sandusky Star Journal* (Sandusky, OH), July 25, 1916.

43. "21 Dead, 9 Hurt in Tunnel Disaster," *Elyria Evening Telegram* (Elyria, OH), July 26, 1916.

44. Quoted in James, *The Real McCoy*, p. 92.

45. Gaius Chamberlain, "Garrett Morgan."

46. Quoted in Gary R. Kremer, ed., *George Washington Carver in His Own Words*. Columbia, MO: University of Missouri Press, 1991, p. 20.

47. Quoted in B.D. Mayberry, ed., *A George Washington Carver Handbook*. Montgomery, AL: New South, 2007, p. 13.

48. Quoted in Mayberry, *A George Washington Carver Handbook*, p. 14.

49. Quoted in Mayberry, *A George Washington Carver Handbook*, p. 12.

50. Quoted in Jack Rummel, *African-American Social Leaders and Activists*. New York, NY: Facts on File, 2011, p. 26

51. Charles Van Doren, ed., *Webster's American Biographies*. Springfield, MA: G. & C. Merriam, 1974, p. 182.

52. "George Washington Carver," *Reno Evening Gazette* (Reno, NV), January 7, 1943.

Chapter Five: Changing Attitudes, Changing Technology

53. Quoted in "Income Gap Between Blacks, Whites Expands," NPR, November 13, 2007. www.npr.org/templates/story/story.php?storyId=16257374.

54. Quoted in Dave Kenney, *Minnesota Goes to War: The Home Front During World War II*. St. Paul, MN: Minnesota Historical Society, 2005, p. 149.

55. Quoted in Jim Jones, "Thermo King Owes a Lot to Founder's Hot Idea," *Minneapolis Star and Tribune*, June 15, 1987, p. 1M.

56. "They Had a Dream," *New Castle News* (New Castle, PA), January 24, 1970, p. 3.

57. Quoted in Kenney, *Minnesota Goes to War*, p. 150.

58. "Device Guarantees Fresh Vegetables," *New Castle News* (New Castle, PA), April 12, 1951.

59. "DePauw to Graduate 6th in Family," *Anderson Herald* (Anderson, IN), May 22, 1970.

60. Quoted in "*Sun-Times* Features One-Time 'Chicagoan of the Year,' Percy Lavon Julian '20," DePauw University, February 5, 2007. www.depauw.edu/news/index.asp?id=18849.

61. "Triton Names Hall for Dr. Percy Julian," *News-Journal* (Chicago, IL), April 14, 1976.

62. Quoted in Patents.com, "T-shirt with Removable Sleeves Convertible to a Hat," accessed January 18, 2017. patents.com/us-d499857.html.

FOR MORE INFORMATION

Books

Abdul-Jabbar, Kareem, and Alan
Steinberg. *Black Profiles in
Courage*. New York, NY:
Morrow, 1996.
This book is an interesting account
of important African Americans
throughout history, including
several inventors.

Bundles, A'Lelia Perry. *On Her Own
Ground: The Life and Times of
Madam C.J. Walker*. New York,
NY: Scribner, 2001.
This detailed biography of Madam
Walker was researched and writ-
ten by one of her descendants.

Harness, Cheryl. *The Ground-
Breaking, Chance-Taking Life
of George Washington Carver
and Science and Invention
in America*. Washington, DC:
National Geographic, 2008.
A biographical account of Carver
that puts his work in the context
of contemporary technology,
this work is a great expansion on
Carver's incredible work and life.

James, Portia P. *The Real McCoy:
African American Invention
and Innovation, 1619–1930*.
Washington, DC: Smithsonian, 1989.
Well illustrated and informative,
this book focuses on black inven-
tors and scientists throughout
American history.

Mazurkiewicz, Margaret, ed.
*Contemporary Black Biography.
Volume 93: Profiles from the
International Black Community*.
Detroit, MI: Gale, 2012.
This book is part of a larger series
that focuses on influential and
important African Americans
throughout history.

Sullivan, Otha Richard. *African
American Women Scientists and
Inventors*. New York, NY:
Wiley, 2001.
This book is a great biography of
black women in the sciences and
includes information on Madam
C.J. Walker and other
female inventors.

Walker, Jonathan. *Granville Taylor
Woods: The First Black American
Who Was Granted Forty-Nine
Patents*. Bloomington, IN:
Xlibris, 2012.
This detailed historical text
focuses on Woods's work and his
numerous patents; it is geared
toward young scholars.

Websites

Famous African American Inventors (teacher.scholastic.com/activities/bhistory/inventors)
This website consists of a good list of well-known and unknown African American inventors, with links to further information about many of them and their inventions.

Famous Black Inventors (www.black-inventor.com)
This useful website has a great deal of information about African American inventors from all time periods, and it is organized like an encyclopedia.

"Garrett A. Morgan" (ech.case.edu/cgi/article.pl?id=MGA)
Case Western Reserve University, a prestigious school, compiled an encyclopedia of influential Cleveland residents; its entry on Garrett Morgan is a useful sketch of his life.

NOVA: "Forgotten Genius" (www.pbs.org/wgbh/nova/Julian)
This website is a companion to a documentary about the life of Percy Julian, and it includes biographical information with links to other sites.

"20 Black Inventions Over the Last 100 Years You May Not Know" (atlantablackstar.com/2013/10/23/100-black-inventions-over-the-last-100-years-you-may-not-know-part-1)
This brief list provides insight about a number of African American inventors and their inventions; it also includes numerous pictures of the creators and their creations.

INDEX

PICTURE CREDITS

ABOUT THE AUTHOR

Sophie Washburne has been a freelance writer and editor of young adult and adult books for more than 10 years. She travels extensively with her husband, Alan. When they are not traveling, they live in Wales with their cat, Zoe. Sophie enjoys doing crafts and cooking when she has spare time. She is happy computer technology created laptops so she can write no matter where she is in the world.